A Joyful Way of Being

A Joyful Way of Being

Rediscovering Creative Expression in the Middle of Life

BrittMarie Eksell

SHE WRITES PRESS

Published in 2026 by
She Writes Press, an imprint of The Stable Book Group

32 Court Street, Suite 2109
Brooklyn, NY 11201
https://shewritespress.com

The Library of Congress Control Number is available upon request.
ISBN: 979-8-89636-106-0
eISBN: 979-8-89636-107-7

Interior designer: Katherine Lloyd, The DESK
Printed in the United States

Names and identifying characteristics have been changed to protect the privacy of certain individuals.

To the memory of my parents,
and to my teachers, with deep appreciation

Contents

Foreword

By Dr. Christiane Manzella

Creativity is often misunderstood. It is frequently seen as a talent—something you either have or don't. But in my years of working with students, researchers, and clinicians in the field of psychology, I have come to recognize creativity as something much deeper: a means of emotional expression, a bridge to self-discovery, and a powerful tool for transformation. Nowhere have I seen this truth more clearly than in the work of BrittMarie Eksell.

I first encountered BrittMarie's teaching while observing a graduate seminar for psychology students. What struck me immediately was not just the depth of knowledge being shared but the way in which students were actively engaging with creativity as a means of understanding human experience. Through practical exercises, thoughtful discussion, and an invitation to explore their own expressive capacities, students were uncovering new ways to connect with themselves and with others. It was evident that this was not just an academic pursuit—it was a lived experience of transformation.

This book is an extension of that work. It offers not only insights into the role of creativity in personal growth but also a hands-on approach to creative engagement. For many, the idea of exploring creativity can feel intimidating. But as BrittMarie so beautifully illustrates, creativity is not about mastering a craft—it is about allowing oneself to step into possibility, to play, to explore. The exercises and reflections found in these pages will encourage even the most hesitant among us to rediscover the joy of making and expressing.

Beyond the academic setting, the importance of this work extends far into the realm of everyday life. As a professor, I have seen how creativity can be a vital tool in therapy, in navigating life transitions, and in fostering resilience. I have also seen how many people, particularly adults, struggle with self-doubt when it comes to creative expression. This book meets those doubts with encouragement, offering a welcoming space for anyone—whether student, professional, or simply curious seeker—to explore creativity as a pathway to emotional well-being.

I encourage you to approach this book with openness and curiosity. Whether you are a therapist seeking new ways to engage clients, a student eager to deepen their understanding of human experience, or someone looking to reconnect with their own creativity, you will find inspiration and practical guidance within these pages. A life-changing perspective. To see and to feel seen—whether by trees, images, or art—is a profound experience. When the object of our vision seems to respond, a dialogue begins. I have personally experienced this back-and-forth essence of creativity—and I know it has the power to transform us.

It is with great admiration for BrittMarie's work and its impact that I invite you to begin this journey. I have no doubt that you, like the many students who have been fortunate enough to learn from BrittMarie in the classroom, will find your creative voice along the way, and in doing so uncover new possibilities for joy, healing, and personal growth.

Introduction

We live in a time when most of us reach midlife and beyond, remaining healthy, physically and mentally active, and not slowing down much if at all. As we notice shifts in our daily routines during midlife, we find a new space after years of responsibilities, work, and social commitments. This period might involve retirement, early leave from work, or the departure of grown children. We may face the loss of a partner or parents, leaving us seeking new meaning, purpose, and joy.

As a teenager, I read Bertrand Russell's words on old age: "It is the time when you begin to look backward to the time that you used to look forward to." This resonated with me as a challenge. Now, in later life, I believe we continue to look forward to new learning and adventures. Old age is to be embraced and celebrated for its potential. It's a time to prioritize stillness and inner peace, allowing us to listen to our own creative voice and find deeper joy.

This book connects you to your inner creative expression and wisdom, offering new revelations and habits. It fosters a renewal of play, complemented by tools like journals, meditation, and therapy. *A Joyful Way of Being* uses images to provide a holistic, sensory experience for exploring emotions. It addresses questions such as:

- Where do I find inspiration for renewal at midlife?
- How can I use creativity to tap into my feelings?
- Why is it important to connect to play again at my age?
- How can I overcome fear and reluctance about making changes in my life?

These questions are answered through stories from patients and workshop participants I've worked with as an art therapist and health psychologist focused on creativity. While not delving deeply into neuroscience, I share physiological and psychological findings from my research on creativity and health, with references for further reading.

This book is for those who are transitioning through different stages of midlife and want to learn about themselves and find ways to express their emotions, dreams, and thoughts, discovering a more joyful way of being.

How to Use This Book

No background or previous experience in creative art-making is needed to enjoy this book. You can move through it in different ways: read chapters that speak to you first, focus on the images and comments, or follow each chapter sequentially. Each chapter includes exercises with easy-to-follow instructions, open to your interpretation and choice of creative medium. Set aside extra time for contemplation and dialogue with your artwork. Patience and practice are key to the creative process, which varies for everyone.

My hope is that this book opens a doorway to curiosity in your creative self, leading you to inspiration and a jubilant path. Reading responses to exercise prompts may reawaken your creative visions. Sharing our stories enriches our well-being. Yet, you have something unique to express. This artful journey encourages you to experience the world with wonder, awe, and magic throughout the second half of life, where your creative spirit thrives.

Letting go of certainties leads to openness; openness leads to revelation; revelation leads to discovery; discovery leads to enlargement.

—James Hollis, *Finding Meaning in the Second Half of Life*

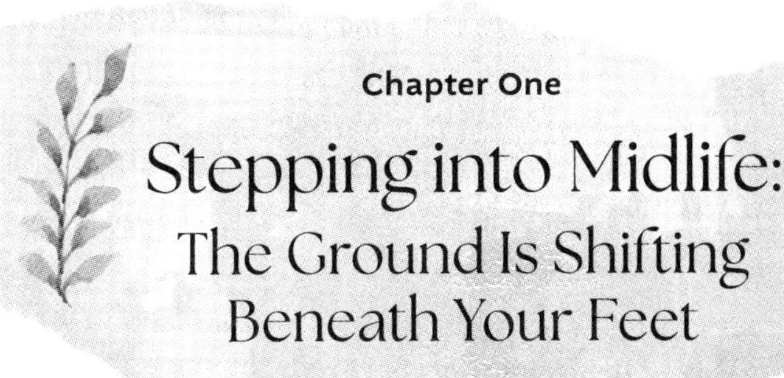

Chapter One

Stepping into Midlife: The Ground Is Shifting Beneath Your Feet

Midway along life's journey,
I woke to find myself in a dark wood.

—Dante Alighieri, *Inferno, Canto I*

There comes a time, slowly, almost imperceptibly, when we begin to ask ourselves: What is the meaning of my life? Where am I going? What have I learned about myself? Why have I lost my joy and enthusiasm? What am I willing to leave behind so I can become more of my true self? Once these thoughts have entered our mind, there is no turning back. There is one way, and that is forward, forward to the only journey that ultimately matters, the journey inward.

For many of us, these questions typically emerge at midlife. Prior to this time, we have been busy raising families, working, traveling, paying bills, and volunteering, leaving us with little time to go inward and seek answers to what we want out of our life's journey. How simple it would be if we could just turn a page in our book at midlife and write a new chapter at age fifty or sixty with the headings "Before" and "After." Alas, it is not that easy.

The challenge of making a significant transition—beginning a second (or third) career, leaving a relationship, moving to a different city or country, becoming a grandparent, going back to school, pursuing a passion—can be a rocky process. Some people turn to a therapist, a support group, their religious leaders, a life coach, or midlife retreat centers. We may start new exercise routines and play brain-training games, hoping to add more years to our lives and more life and lightness to our years. All good tools, but *A Joyful Way of Being* will introduce another option for how to manage this transition in a daily or weekly practice: a creative exercise that can be done in the privacy of our home and won't cost anything except a few inexpensive art materials.

From Pain to Process to Purpose

What most of us fail to recognize is that midlife can become a time of tremendous personal growth and the unleashing of our true purpose during our next chapters. Even the most outwardly successful and happy people start to question the meaning of their life as they shift out of primary careers or end other long-time pursuits, such as childrearing or volunteer commitments. Many of us have checked all the boxes—we've obtained a certain education, become financially comfortable, nurtured a loyal set of friends, and are attentive to loving family members. It feels like we've created a strong foundation for a future life of stress-free existence.

Then our world gets rocked by the loss of a spouse, a parent, or a sibling, or maybe we have a health scare of our own. We begin to wonder how to fill our days with a sense of meaning, fulfillment, and joy. The inevitable pains of life may have taken away our ability to be playful and curious in the world, and we struggle to find something that will engage our minds and hearts. The process of finding purpose at midlife can feel like we're walking through the dark woods, as Dante writes.

"Life is difficult" is the first line in *The New York Times* bestseller *The Road Less Traveled* by M. Scott Peck. This is his way of saying that it can be a long and winding path to becoming your own true self. I recall when reading Peck's book, both the sense of surprise and relief that he affirmed my anxiety around big transitions. I wasn't in midlife yet, but I was deeply in the process of navigating personal changes, disappointments, and uncertainties that contributed to my inability to find joy and fulfillment. I had not yet learned that pain can be a wake-up call to pursue a new road that will get us closer to our purpose. Pain, when physiological, can be a calling from our body trying to connect to us, trying to let us know something is going on that may need our attention.

Pain is indeed one of the most important wake-up calls for our well-being. When ignored or not taken seriously, it may change our life in a way that is not life-enhancing, but rather life-threatening. In my forties, I suffered tremendous pain from an inflamed appendix. At the time, I was on a month-long hike in a Midwest forest. Trying my best to ignore the pain and continue the hike, I finally fainted from exhaustion. Fortunately, I was airlifted to the closest hospital, where I was told that it was a miracle that I was still alive after having experienced a ruptured appendix more than a week ago. Even though I believed that I had a deep connection with my body, there was still much to learn. Today, I try to think of my body as my very best friend, wherein I live, and am determined to treat this body with the highest respect and admiration. Something new to learn every day.

In addition to physiological pain, we all experience from time to time psychological pain and confusion. The pain of anxiety, doubt, and darkness is not so easy to put aside, to ignore, or to understand. After World War II, psychology became an accepted science that was mostly devoted to healing and repairing, with a focus on various disease models. In other words, psychological treatment was focused on minimizing the effects of such things as historical and present mental confusion, depression, and lack of self-worth. However, and fortunately for our future, by the 1990s, a new branch of psychology emerged: positive psychology.

This branch of psychology proposes a shift from treating mental illness to preventing these pathologies from arising, even when we feel that life is meaningless, barren, or when we cannot find joy in that which used to bring us such satisfaction. That said, it does in no way imply that we can cure a serious physical or psychological health problem with an optimistic outlook. But wherever life may find us, by connecting to ourselves on a deeper level, we may find unexpected support from our continued inner energy that may awaken us to finding a glimmer of hope and joy even in the darkest of circumstances.

The movement toward positive psychology around the shift of the millennium was greatly supported by well-known psychologists such as Martin E. P. Seligman, Mihaly Csikszentmihalyi, and James E. Pennebaker, among many others. They wrote about how an optimistic outlook and hope affect health, what constitutes wisdom, and how talent and creativity come to fruition. Their hope was that their research would reveal a science that would support and understand factors that allow individuals, communities, and societies to flourish.

Focusing on positive qualities to enhance equanimity and joy is nothing new. Throughout the ages, the philosophical focus on virtue, beauty, and creativity can be traced back to Athens in the fifth century BC, Florence in the fifth century, and Victorian England, all of which affirmed honor, discipline, and duty as central to enjoying a well-lived life.

Today, maybe more than ever before, when we are faced with overwhelm and exhaustion from both natural and man-made disasters, it is not unusual that we also feel a tumultuous transition within ourselves. So, how do we look at the world around us with optimism and hope? We are all acting as a conduit for the effects of that which is taking place in our environment. The projection of anxieties both from without and from within is noted. We may notice we feel more tired than usual, or our focus and alertness are not so present, even if on an unconscious level. This is the time when it is extra helpful for our health of mind, hope, and well-being to move even further within.

By connecting to the joy that lies in wait for all of us, the process of moving into the flow of creativity will happen one step at a time . . . even when we hear that silent voice within us that is putting its heels down, calling out doubts, insecurities, and any kind of interference that prevent us from following our deeper calling. That is when we go even deeper. That is when we open ourselves to what is truly calling us to move forward with joy and purpose. We may not have a word for our unique calling, but we know what feels right in the process of our creative path. Without judgment we move forward to something that speaks to us loudly, a voice that we recognize as coming from within. Your own unique voice has always been with you but may not always have been heard or noticed. This is the voice that will bring both joy and purpose to the road ahead.

I read *The Road Less Traveled* at a time in my life when I was struggling to find my true self. I had recently moved from Sweden to New York, having left a well-paid position as an assistant actuary in a large corporation to become an art student at Pratt Institute. This was not the most financially intelligent career change! Although somewhere inside me, I knew that I would let my creative side suffer if I stayed analyzing statistics and risk assessment in an office all day.

My parents were not happy with my decision. I disappointed them, both by giving up what they thought would turn into a lucrative career and by leaving Sweden and not knowing when or if I would ever return. I still hear my mother's voice: "I forgive you, but I will never understand you." That was very painful to hear at the time. Later in life, after studying the philosophy of Carl Jung and Joseph Campbell, I was able to look back with more insight and compassion on the transition of leaving my parents' home. I learned that we all go through what used to be called rites of passage and that this can happen throughout different periods in our lives. Today, we have different names for these transitions, which, around our fifties or earlier, is often called a "midlife crisis." Although crisis may have a negative connotation, the crisis or transition can be one of the most important calls for our inner growth potential toward a meaningful life.

I loved being a student at Pratt and exploring all kinds of artistic projects, but I also felt the ache of separation from my family and was anxious when the high expectations I had for myself were rarely met. I was desperate to feel grounded somehow. Being an art student, I started playing around with an image of myself as a mountain goat, balancing on spiking cliff heights while suspended in midair, where predators abounded and the abyss was always close by. When I shared this image with my therapist, she asked me to close my eyes and imagine that I was safely walking in a beautiful meadow deep in the comfort of a surrounding valley. I instantly imagined I was like Bambi, scrambling to get my legs underneath me to have something to hold on to. The beautiful valley wasn't quite within reach yet, but keeping this image in my mind helped me to continue to pursue new heights and become more comfortable with meeting difficult challenges, primarily trusting in myself that I could become a creative artist. This small act of image-making was my first realization that art is a lens into what I am feeling inside, and acknowledging those emotions cleared the path for me to pursue my greater purpose.

One of the great benefits of aging is that we have the confidence to become more of who we truly are, rather than trying to fit into a set of boxes filled with expectations and projections that are not always of our own making. Instead of looking at midlife as a decline into less of life, we can shift our minds to be open to continuous personal growth and a courageous choice to make changes. As the writer Anaïs Nin wrote in her book *The Diary of Anais Nin*, "Life shrinks or expands in proportion to one's courage."

When I was a student at Pratt, my purpose was to become a textile designer. And yet, that wasn't the end of my art expression in the world. After about a decade of working as a textile artist, my intention changed. A new calling led me to pursue a career as an art therapist. And with more time, another purpose appeared: to earn a doctorate in health psychology. If on the exterior our purposes tend to appear rather varied, there is often a thread underneath that binds them all together like a flowing river with its larger and lesser tributaries. My river has always flowed in the direction of art and images in some form, naturally finding its own way. When we think about our friends or family, we might notice that each of us has that unique river of our own. A river that is constantly moving forward, even when we cannot see what will meet us around the bend but can only catch glimpses of what may lie ahead.

The beauty of midlife is that we can look back and begin to find that flowing thread that has moved us along in our path and will move us forward into the future. This may require stepping outside of our comfort zone and listening to the voice from our soul. It does not follow that we change our family situation or uproot ourselves by moving to an ashram in India to find our purpose. All that we are asking from ourselves is that we have the courage to slowly open to an awareness that there is a purpose for us. A caveat here is that purpose itself does not necessarily mean something "larger than life." We don't have to suddenly become known for climbing Mount Everest after age seventy or eighty; we don't have to write a best-selling novel or become a superhero on the tennis or pickleball court.

We cannot force this discovery through rational thinking and words only, but rather by letting feelings, sensations, and images help guide us to an understanding of where we have been and imagining where we are going. In other words, we must *live our experiences and emotions* to know what truly matters.

Art as the Lens to Our Inner Journey

Many midlife self-help practices, such as journaling or talk therapy, rely on words to uncover and express deeper emotions. Choosing words to express ourselves requires a high level of conscious thinking and a quick judgment call on our part to choose "the right word." In doing so, we may block out our inner soul, which lies in our subconscious feelings. Forming an image on the page using our hands and a simple tool like a pencil requires us to be naturally intuitive and free flowing and provides a direct conduit into our feelings and soul.

Suleika Jaouad, *New York Times* best-selling author of *Between Two Kingdoms*, in which she writes about her cancer journey, says that she often cannot find the words that depict the anger, fear, pain, and joy in her journey—despite being a published author! She often turns to creating small pieces of art—paintings, embroidery, sketches—to process her feelings. "When I was young, I would go up to my mom's studio in the attic of our house. I would experiment with charcoal sticks and gouache paints and papier-mâché (i.e., I made giant, glorious messes). At that age, creativity felt joyous, egoless, purely fun." Suleika, like many of us, may have lost the ability to use creativity and art in a joyful and revealing way.

Creativity is not bound to a certain age in life, and our ability to access it does not diminish with the passage of time. Too many people adopt the notion that art is a mode of expression used only by the young, and that our "creativity muscle" becomes weaker as decades pass by. This thinking is all wrong and a much too common, misguided obstacle to our journey! Creativity is something that deepens and becomes richer with age.

You are already using art to express yourself and your emotions. Think of how you take pictures with your smartphone to share your views of the world and your life. Most people with a phone are photographers today, and it has become the lens through which we view the world and ourselves. Statistics indicate that ninety-two million selfies are taken every day. And billions more photos are taken across devices on a regular basis. While most of those images depict a surface moment of experience, we seldom stop to ask what lies underneath the image. What emotions are we conveying in our images, which are rarely shared either with oneself or with others?

During a period when Carl Jung, the famed Swiss psychiatrist and founder of analytical psychology, was going through a deep transition himself, he turned to the practice of making circular drawings of the mandala. The mandala (a Sanskrit word for "circle") is a basic form that can be found in many parts of nature, including animals. The symbolism of a circle can further be found in many cultures. The Aztec calendars, Navajo and Tibetan sand paintings, and Gothic cathedral rose windows are but a few examples. Jung felt that the protective, enclosing circle provided a space where he could superimpose his sometimes chaotic stream of thoughts. It was a place where his mind's fast-moving stream could be held in check, and at the same time, his imposed image provided creative guidance to further insight. He wrote:

> *. . . I sketched every morning in a notebook a small circular drawing—a mandala. Only gradually did I discover what the mandala really is: "Formation, Transformation,*

> *eternal Mind's eternal recreation." . . . In them I saw the self—that is, my whole being—actively at work.*

Several years ago, during a weeklong wilderness expedition with eco-psychologist and wilderness guide Bill Plotkin, I decided to create a mandala in my notebook. One day, after being thoroughly briefed on safety precautions, our assignment was to spend the entire day alone in the deep woods. The challenge was significant—not just the solitude, but the knowledge that grizzly and black bears had recently emerged from hibernation with their cubs. Despite my initial trepidation, I learned to trust my instincts, gradually loosening the grip of fear imposed by my mind.

As Jung described, the mandala became a reflection of the shift in consciousness I was undergoing. Throughout my life, nature had always been my grounding force—a teacher, a friend, a silent and trusted guide. Drawing and painting my mandala in the heart of the wilderness, I felt a profound sense of safety, as if held within the circle I had created. The only sounds around me were the rhythmic flow of a nearby river, the wind moving through the trees, and the vast embrace of silence. When I finished my mandala and contemplated the images that had emerged, a deep sense of connection settled over me—a connection to nature, to the world, and to the intricate web of experiences that shape our daily lives.

However, after years of living in a fast-paced, stressful city and navigating the slow, painful unraveling of a long-term marriage, both my mental and physical energy had begun to wane. As an artist and psychologist who had spent years examining my own life through therapy, I understood the necessity of facing pain and disappointment head-on—moving through them rather than being consumed by them. Every life presents new challenges, but when we accept our deepest fears as part of our growth, they become the very force that propels us toward creative renewal. Without challenge, there is no transformation. Without action, no reaction. And without creative expression, we remain trapped, unable to evolve into our fullest potential.

One of the first warm-up exercises I do when conducting an art-making workshop is to ask the participants to create a self-portrait without using a mirror. This may seem daunting at first and is often met with a gasp of fear. However, without the distraction of a mirror, but simply from touching and feeling their head and hair, the exercise becomes an experience of self-discovery and sometimes surprise. The purpose is not to have the participants make an accurate image of themselves, but rather to take time to connect to their *feelings* and let them come forward on the paper in front of them.

The colors in a self-portrait are chosen from the inner voice rather than from the conscious mind. I also ask them to cut out images from a magazine to add to their portrait, along with a title. For many people, what emerges are images that reflect memories that are long held and almost forgotten, but receive a new meaning based on their changing perspectives as they go through life. There is a sense of gratitude expressed by most of the participants when they have experienced a feeling of reuniting with memories as if they were old friends, and that are still there for them today.

Elsa was a quiet and soft-spoken woman in her mid-fifties who hesitated to start on her self-portrait, but the more she put down on her paper, there was nothing that would stop her enthusiastic creativity. After Elsa had finished, she titled her painting *Can This Be Me?* As the title suggests, her painting was a surprise to her:

> *When making my self-portrait I was somewhat surprised to see that I had made the conscious decision to relegate an important part away from the rest of me . . . so it made me*

realize that no matter how much self-reflection one makes, people can continue to discover and rediscover part of themselves every day no matter what age.

Embarking on the creative journey of using art as a lens into your soul is not meant to produce a piece of skilled museum art. Nor should it be hung on your refrigerator next to the grocery shopping list. It is designed to be our art alone, not to be shared with anybody else. When you commit to making art as a regular practice, you learn how to look inside, listen to your soul, and become more comfortable with your own creativity. You will soon find that your artwork will be like that spellbinding novel or documentary that you read, where you cannot wait to see what is on the next page. And when you finally finish the story, you wish that there were more pages. You have become so involved in the story and its riches of ups and downs that you want to learn more. And so it is with your life; the more we draw, paint, photograph, or sculpt, the more we use our creative energy, there is a new world that opens to us.

Exercise: Journey into Our Current Self

Warm-up Writing:

Spend three minutes writing:

- As a child, what did you see yourself doing as an adult?
- Name the bends in your river that moved you to a new calling.

Materials:

Drawing pad (9 x12 inches or larger)
Colored pencils, crayons, and watercolors

Instructions:

1. On a large sheet of paper, begin by drawing a face form that represents your personal shape—this could be oval, round, or square, and from a front view.
2. Loosely follow these proportions as you add features to your face:
    - Place the **eyes** about halfway between the tip of your chin and the top of your head.
    - The **tip of the nose** sits halfway between the eyes and the chin.
    - The **mouth** is halfway between the nose and the chin.
    - Draw the **hair** as a shape—think of it as volume and form rather than individual strands.
    - If you choose to add **ears**, they typically stretch from the eye line to the bottom of the nose.
3. Use crayons to draw simple lines representing the **neck and shoulders**.

4. Now it's time to fully **color in your shape** using crayons or watercolor—choose any tones, shades, or colors that come to mind. Think of the expressive colors and bold forms of **Fauvism** or **Matisse.** (You can search their names online for inspiration.)

This may be a new experience: You're making a self-portrait without looking at a photo or a mirror. Instead, gently feel around your head and face with your hands to get a sense of shape. Let your memories of your own reflection guide the rest.

To increase your awareness of **touch**, try closing your eyes—or even sitting in the dark—as you explore the contours of your face. Without sight, your sense of touch becomes more vivid.

Most of all, **try not to judge your artwork**. This isn't about accuracy. Enjoy the process. Let yourself discover how a color, a shape, or a line might offer another way of **seeing yourself**. When we go beyond what we first encounter visually—when imagination invites us deeper—we often meet new aspects of ourselves. This is where the joy begins.

Exercise Reflection:

What does each color mean to you? What thoughts, feelings, or memories come forward as you spend a few moments with each color? Make a list of your colors and write a short poem from them.

Examples by a group of participants:

Red: fire, anger, joy, warmth, cozy, home, fall, what I like to surround myself with in the fall and winter
White: nothing, has all my love in the calm of my day
Orange: lukewarm, citrus, sun in the afternoon, beautiful silk
Yellow: happy, safe, joy, sun at midday

Green: secure, surrounds me calmly, light green is clear, washes my eyes
Blue: cool, water running in the pool, hard, royal, patriarchy
Violet: plum, mohair sweater in the fall, regal, old, sacred
Brown: warm, Mother Earth, timeless
Black: the night, deep water crossing the ocean

Sharing from a workshop participant:

It was with ease that the instructor encouraged us in the understanding of color and on to painting a self-portrait and feeling comfortable with the process. By using pictures of Matisse's Fauvist paintings, she also allowed us to get out of the conventional thought mode that everything must look a certain established way but rather be allowed to express more of the inner energies.

It is comforting and invites sharing when we are seated with more than one person around each table. But I noticed how even those "grown-ups" wanted the project to go fast—to be done rather than to explore and be amazed by the mystery of color.

Giggles and funny comments about their own work. But then it became still and peaceful when we had some time to write about what the colors meant to us and to try to remember why we chose them. It awakened something in me. Not sure yet. It will take some time.

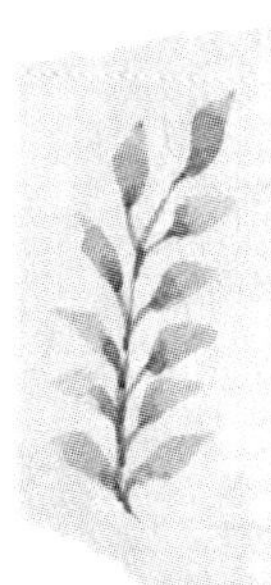

Chapter Two

Developing Your Inner Artist

Becoming human means discovering our fullness and learning to live from it. This involves bringing forth more of who we really are and becoming more available to whatever life presents.

—John Welwood

You may be asking yourself, "Is there an inner artist in me? If so, why have I not met this artist earlier in my life, or have I? Can I remember any creative activities I did, and how I felt about those once completed?" There likely is more than one answer to these questions, and reflecting on your experience with art as a child will provide insights into how you can bring back that sense of joy and wonder into your life today.

Think back to the times when you scribbled a drawing for the first time as a toddler, constructed a pot out of playdough, or made a fort out of an old appliance box. You were so proud to share your creations with your parents or siblings. Your inner child was strongly connected to that instinctual process. When you spend time on this "memory walk," visualizations may bring up emotions such as excitement and wonder. This could be a good time to bring out a drawing or painting that you made as a child that has survived somewhere in your archives.

My mother kept a diary of her children's development from birth until about the age of seven. During a recent move, I was happy to find that the diary is still with me after all these years. It was delightful to become the reader of my early story, to look back and think about the kind of child I was at that time. There are a few photographs in the diary, but mostly it contains my mother's writing about milestone developments, setbacks, and progress. Today, most parents have short videos of their children, often taken with a smartphone. I find tremendous joy in watching the videos on my phone of my niece's two toddlers as they grow and interact. On some level, these visual records bring back the experiences of once having been a child ourselves, when "play" was our main activity for the day.

While recently flipping through my well-traveled diary, I came across a charming drawing from when I was five years old. It depicts a simple and joyful outdoor picnic scene. The picture features a bright yellow sun shining in the sky, with a few wavy lines representing clouds. On the left, there is a tree with green leaves, drawn with expressive, uneven lines, suggesting a lively natural setting. In the center, a green picnic blanket is laid out on the grass with a child resting on it. She has curly yellow hair and wears a red skirt and yellow top, all drawn with a simplistic yet endearing style typical of early childhood artwork. On the blanket are picnic items, including a slice of cake, a few cups, berries, and small fruits. To the right in the picture, another child, wearing a dark blue dress, stands on the grass. Their faces are depicted with two dots for eyes and a simple mouth, giving them an expressive but minimalistic look. In large, quirky letters, I had titled it: *We Are Having a Picnic.* Seeing it now, I am instantly transported back to the excitement of planning what to bring for our backyard picnic!

Throughout my early work as an art therapist, I often worked with young children. Their sense of clarity, color combinations, and balance in composition is so instinctively well-crafted because they haven't adopted the "inner critic" of most adults. Many of us are taught that composition is difficult and that it takes years of practice to learn. But when we can allow ourselves to simply "be" with the voice of our own creative lens, composition has a natural ease and flow. From the moment we are born, we are composers, as is evident in my early yet well-balanced picnic picture of both colors and objects.

Too often, I see where people's inborn instinct for expression is overtaken by their conscious minds. What we may not realize is that our expressive instinct is still within us. We have the capacity to change, to grow, and transform with our authentic creative imagination at the core of every human being. But we may have some work ahead of us, namely, to tear away all the protective layers that we have surrounded ourselves with throughout our lives. These are the layers that tell us that we are not good enough, that compare us to others, and that lack the courage to meet our creative selves. We need to shed these layers! The only thing that matters is to embrace our authentic, original creative self that is trying to awaken. A fair amount of patience, creative experimentation, and willingness will get us there! Good things will happen to all of us when we take charge of our creative selves, when creative joy becomes our way of being.

As we grow into adults, society conditions us to believe that art-making is only intended for a small, esoteric, and elite group of truly talented individuals. Studies on creative development in children have found that around the time they enter fourth or fifth grade, it is not unusual for them to experience what is often referred to as a creative slump. One of my friends had noticed this slump in her son Daniel. He used to be very proud of the drawings he brought home from school in second grade.

Attaching them to the refrigerator, he would look at them with joy and point to the bright green polka dots on a tractor with stars and suns flying around the page. By fifth grade, the drawings no longer came back home. Daniel felt that the creative class was not so much fun anymore: "Mom, you should see the way Laura and John draw. Their paintings look really real . . . I am not very creative."

We experience free-flowing creativity in childhood but soon begin to feel the shame and pain of comparison as we share our work in the world. How can we embrace play and joy as adults if we have tied our creative self-worth to those early comparative memories? The good news is that our innate ability to express ourselves creatively does not disappear. Our creative voice cannot be silenced for all time. It is the light within that will always remain lit, whether we are conscious of this or not. Becoming aware of how and when we see the world through our artful lens is important not only in the way we creatively express our emotions, but also in how it taps into the part of ourselves that allows for our individual differences, gratitude, and courage.

When I first met Eleanor, she was in her late forties. Tall, slender, and athletic, she often enjoyed walking in the mountains behind her home with her constant companion, a Labrador dog named Bear. Besides being an excellent healer, Eleanor was also a dancer and traveled frequently to perform. For the last two decades, she had been working with patients whose physical problems were not solved by traditional medicine. Ironically, she suffered from chronic back pain. But when it came to her own healing, Eleanor was not able to give herself the same attention to care and comfort that she imparted to her patients.

As a child, Eleanor had spent the summers with her family at their summer residence close to a beach where she loved to play and swim. One of her favorite experiences was to swim where she could see the bottom of the lake, the moving sea grass, and the sun faintly coming through from above. I suggested to Eleanor that she return to her childhood wonder, where she was the one being looked after, and where carefree play was a matter of joy and exploration. Through her art-making, Eleanor began to explore why she wasn't caring for and supporting herself, and she imagined what it would feel like once she did.

In a deeply symbolic and emotionally resonant drawing, she expressed the healing power of nature as she envisioned herself as a whale peacefully moving through water. The drawing portrays an uplifting scene where she is embraced by water and bathed in the sun's warmth, finding solace and healing in the elements. The whale is supporting a small human figure, who is lying comfortably on their back, as if surrendering to the water's care. The sun, glowing warmly in the background, is depicted in vibrant yellow and orange hues, radiating long, expressive rays that reach out across the sky. This element may symbolize healing energy, a source of life that provides both physical and spiritual warmth.

Through this drawing, Eleanor conveys a powerful emotional landscape—her desire for healing, her deep connection to nature, and the sense of peace she finds in the embrace of the ocean and sun. This may be seen as a testament to the transformative power of creative expression in processing illness and finding inner strength. Eleanor titled her painting *I Am Swimming, I Am Safe, Light and Sound by the Whale Goddess.* She said:

> *After years of supporting others, I think this is the first time that I myself truly feel supported. I am the whale supported by the water in which I am swimming with no end in sight; I am not alone. The light of the sun has found me even though below and under water but still close to the surface. I had no expectations from this . . . difficult*

> *to explain with words, but I believe I can feel the healing aspect from the rays reaching down through the water to my back . . . and I will continue swimming . . . I will put this painting in my office to remind me of the supporting Goddess also within me.*

Throughout our different phases of life, our creativity may have been dormant. We put our creativity on hold as we strive to become good students, work diligently to get the best grades, and start a professional life to support our adult lifestyle and household formation. Some of us may have been lucky enough to land a job where creativity of mind and action were appreciated. But many of us have lived with boundaries separating ourselves from expressing creativity. Yet creativity is not like an old tool that rusts and falls into pieces from disuse. When reaching midlife, our artful, creative lens no longer needs to be held back. It is with unbounded joy that we allow the childhood wonder in combination with learned wisdom to guide us on our path forward.

Overcoming the Judgment Roadblock

We don't have to study textile design at Pratt Institute or spend years completing a PhD in psychology like I did to learn how to use art to express ourselves. On the contrary. All we need to do is let go of the self-imposed blocks to creative expression that so many of us have put in front of our creative play. It takes willingness to meet our vulnerable selves, to detach from negative judgment about our efforts, and to proclaim that our scratches and scribblings are not failures but an invitation to our creative process.

Embracing midlife's artful lens requires trusting in the process, no matter how much we feel we are stumbling along. When you begin to realize your own creative potential, the silent dialogue between you and your images will bring you to new heights of awareness and self-fulfillment. Yes, you will encounter obstacles in the process, such as comparisons, judgments, irritations, and general frustrations (I certainly have lived through all of these in my own creative pursuit), but they can be overcome. The simple act of staying in the process of your creative pursuit and being open to what is being presented by your action is when you have *arrived,* rather than striving for something that does not come from your heart.

There is probably nothing that squashes our creative joy more than judgment. How do we overcome these judgments leading to roadblocks and a standstill? Over time, we notice that these voices of interference are just irritating and noisy and can be quickly put behind us. By acknowledging and letting go of this voice of judgment, we begin the transition to a world filled with potential rather than a barricade to our creative joy. When the unnecessary noise does not get the feedback our ego is looking for, those voices will be more and more infrequent and finally disappear.

All of us on a creative journey are learning, striving, questioning, succeeding, and relentlessly continuing into our unknown future. Every time we engage in a creative project, we renew some small part of ourselves. As individuals, we are in a constant flux of renewal, and we slowly learn to become the witness of our own process and evolution. When we accept the thought that we are but the vehicle for the manifestation of our expression, our progress becomes a journey in surprise, reflection, and joy.

Another way to move past our judgmental roadblocks is to incorporate symbols into our creative work—images that hold personal significance or intrigue us because of their history. In our culture, certain symbols, such as a wedding ring, a key, a red rose, or a cross, carry widely recognized meanings.

Carl Jung draws an important distinction between signs and symbols. A sign provides clear information or direction—it tells us what to do or what to expect. For example, a stop sign signals us to halt, and a logo, like the Starbucks emblem, informs us that coffee is available. The icons on a smartphone or computer are also signs, leading us to specific functions or information.

In contrast, symbols go beyond simple meanings; they carry layers of experience and interpretation that evolve over time. Unlike signs, symbols cannot be reduced to a single definition or fixed message. They emerge from the unconscious and invite personal reflection. Rather than something we immediately "understand," a symbol is something we live with, allowing its meaning to unfold gradually.

Throughout written history, the egg has been the symbol for renewal. In mythology, it is not unusual that heroes were not born, but rather came from the egg. The life energy that lies dormant in the egg became important in fertility rites and mystical healing. According to legends and various cultures, eggs were often used at burials along with the bodies to nourish them on their journey to the next life.

In an exercise called "Cracking the Egg," I ask participants to let judgment flow out while leaving behind the creative life energy. Daisy was in her mid-forties when she joined one of my weekend workshops. After finishing a degree in fine art, she had worked as a designer at a well-known graphic firm before becoming a mother of three children. When her children were young, Daisy decided to be a stay-at-home mom and left the design world behind her. As a busy wife and mother, Daisy never found the time to paint. Even though she enjoyed many creative projects with her children, she moved further away from her own creative voice.

On the second day of our meeting, Daisy slowly painted and paused to contemplate her "egg painting." She'd painted an image of herself inside the cracked egg that helped her to find her creative voice again. (Remember, Daisy had trained as an artist, so her egg image is a little more well-formed than most.) She wrote about the experience:

> *I have long felt as if I am blocked by my own thoughts and cannot get out from them. But in painting this egg and cracking the shell, the cracks moved through my head, and I felt a sense of relief in letting both the good and the bad come out without any judgment on either. I just let it happen . . . I put her in a cup and painted some other symbolic messages to support her egg-body . . . I don't think I will ever look at an egg the same again . . . but it was a fun exercise . . . opened up new doors, some earlier memories, and also new insights and a push to pick up my own voice again.*

Even though we may not be aware of the many symbols that we encounter in daily life, they play a profound role in our consciousness and well-being. Symbols are alive within us, shaping how we understand ourselves and the world. They are not just abstract representations; they influence our emotions, guide our growth, and provide meaning to our experiences. They are essential because they connect us to deeper layers of meaning, emotion, and personal transformation. Below are a few reminders of why they are so essential:

Symbols provide psychological and emotional anchors: In times of uncertainty, symbols ground us. Whether it is a family heirloom, a religious emblem, or a personal motif we return to in our art, symbols serve as touchstones for stability and reassurance. They remind us of who we are, where we have been, and what we value, offering a sense of continuity in an ever-changing world.

Symbols enhance creative expression: Art and storytelling rely on symbols to evoke emotions, create layers of meaning, and invite interpretation. They allow creators to communicate beyond words, tapping into universal themes, such as love, loss, transformation, and hope. When we use symbols in our creative process, we engage in an intuitive dialogue with ourselves and our audience.

Symbols guide us through life's transitions: Major life experiences—birth, marriage, loss, personal reinvention—are often marked by symbols. A phoenix represents rebirth, a key symbolizes unlocking potential, and a spiral suggests growth and evolution. These images provide us with a framework for understanding change, making difficult transitions more manageable and meaningful.

Symbols connect us to something greater: Whether spiritual, cultural, or deeply personal, symbols link us to a sense of belonging and purpose. They remind us that our experiences are part of a larger human story, offering comfort, wisdom, and perspective.

Symbols have a timetable of their own: Sometimes we may create an image or use a recurring motif without consciously understanding why. That is perfectly fine. Symbols work on their own timeline. The unconscious reveals when it is ready. The key is to trust the process, allowing ourselves to sit with our symbols, revisit them, and let their meaning evolve naturally.

When you find yourself drawn to a particular symbol—whether intentionally or unexpectedly appearing in your artwork—pause and reflect on what it might be trying to reveal to you. Symbols often carry **layers of meaning**, which can shift depending on where you are in life, your level of self-awareness (which is always evolving), and the cultural or personal associations you bring to them.

Take the example of a **key**. A key can symbolize **access, opportunity, knowledge, or even something locked away**—but its meaning is deeply personal. What does it represent for you at this moment?

In Daisy's painting, a key hangs on the wall behind her, to the right. Yet Daisy's story does not reveal why the key is there or what it means to her. Like many symbols, its significance may not be immediately clear. Sometimes, it takes time before we truly *see* a symbol—not just as an object, but as a message, an invitation, a doorway into deeper self-awareness.

Now, imagine Daisy's painting is **your** painting. What might the key hold for you? Is it unlocking something? Guarding a secret? Offering a choice? Take a moment to sit with it—let it speak to you in its own time.

Embracing Midlife Wisdom

As we approach midlife, all of us have experienced hopes and disappointments, successes and failures, soaring dreams and painful defeats. These challenges have helped us accrue wisdom that we can use to create new road maps for our lives. We learn how to manage tension and anxiety while saving our energy for things that bring us joy. We learn to be selective about our priorities, and we learn to maintain friendship with those who feed our soul. We learn not to allow our desires to be limited by the external world or others' opinions. And maybe more than anything, we learn to appreciate how we've evolved and developed as human beings, while growing in awareness of our unique and special Self.

It has been said that it is most often through challenges that we grow and awaken. The challenges we all face at midlife allow us to become aware of our artful lens and how to use it to stay in touch with our emotions along our journey. Through engagement and exploration in creative activities at midlife, we develop and practice new skills. These are often helpful skills that may foster creative problem-solving in other physical and mental health areas, such as Eleanor recognizing that she needed to give herself an abundance of self-care around her back problem.

When we think about words that may represent our many years of learning by living, the idea may seem daunting. The voice in our head does not know where to begin, what to leave in, and what to leave out. One thought leads to another, and before we know it, the story may not stop at the size of *War and Peace*. A simpler and less time-intensive way to reflect on our accrued wisdom and personal development throughout our lives is to create a story triptych—a set of three images that reflect our journey in the world.

All traditional stories have three parts to them: the beginning, the middle, and the end. An imaginative and creative exercise is to write our own fictional short story, beginning with the first line of popular fairy tales—"Once upon a time"—and imagine ourselves as the hero or heroine on our way out into the world to fulfill a worthwhile quest. In mythology and literature, these types of stories are often referred to as a "hero's journey." The protagonist faces a perceived insurmountable obstacle that is about to crush them. It takes imagination, skill, and courage for them to continue the quest. Using all mental and physical tools available, the protagonist overcomes the obstacle. They can now venture on to a new quest with renewed purpose and confidence. Creating this "hero's journey" triptych reveals the skills and wisdom we've gained to meet any future challenges.

The following is a shortened version of the story made by Suzanne in one of my weekend workshops. Suzanne had worked as a nurse until her mid-forties, when she retired to be a full-time caretaker for her aging parents. Even though Suzanne was the middle child of three, she saw herself as the only "responsible loyal soldier," always available to assist her parents. Suzanne's older brother, who had left home in his early twenties, was married with four children and a full-time lawyer. Her younger sister, who had suffered from various addictions since being a teenager, rarely contacted her parents and never called on her siblings.

Now in her late sixties and her parents having died a few years ago, Suzanne was able to use her free time for creative pursuits. However, after the death of her parents, she no longer felt useful and wondered how she could be of help to others. She felt a sense of anxiety and restlessness that would not go away. Feeling vulnerable without a large circle of friends and close family members to care for, she was afraid that she would be alone. She worried about how to spend the remaining third of her life in a way that would be meaningful and joyous.

Suzanne had previously joined me for a six-week painting course for beginners where she experienced using different art materials. This time, she looked forward to seeing if combining text with images could help open a doorway to her creative process. In using the structure of a traditional story, the three images created by Suzanne into a triptych tell a powerful story of transformation, self-discovery, and emergence from darkness into light. The images collectively depict a journey—one that begins in uncertainty, moves through shifting perceptions, and culminates in self-realization and joy. Here is a description of Suzanne's three images:

- **Image #1:** ***The Light Searcher***
  A solitary figure, their face and much of their body concealed by a deep purple hooded cloak, stands at the edge of darkness. The person, symbolized by vibrant orange hues, is beginning to step forward, drawn toward a source of light ahead. The contrast between shadow and illumination suggests an internal struggle—perhaps between fear and hope, uncertainty and clarity. The light represents the possibility of change, a future that beckons beyond the unknown.

- **Image #2:** ***Perception Ever-Changing***
  The journey continues as the cloaked figure, now seen from behind, faces a group of four men in wide-brimmed hats. Their silhouettes loom against a soft pink background, where morning light gently breaks through. The shift in perspective suggests a reevaluation—perhaps of past influences, authority figures, or societal expectations. The figure is no longer isolated but confronted with the external world, hinting at the evolving nature of perception and the challenges of navigating personal transformation.

- **Image #3:** ***Led by the Stars***
  The final image is one of liberation. The purple hood—the symbol of previous hesitation or protection—is discarded, revealing the full, multilayered essence of the person. Their form radiates vitality, movement, and confidence as they step fully into the light. No longer alone, they are surrounded by others, walking with them in joy

and harmony. The transition from darkness to light is complete, suggesting that the person has embraced their true self, shedding past burdens and stepping into a future guided by inner strength and wisdom.

These three images hold a deeply symbolic visual narrative of courage, awakening, and self-discovery, illustrating the transformative journey of stepping out of fear and into personal empowerment. Suzanne wrote:

Once upon a time, there was a woman who decided to go on a journey to find her sister, who had been kidnapped ten years earlier by a group of bandits. The sister was the light in her life. After several weeks of travel, she felt very tired . . . resting beside a lake, she encountered a young woman who was fixing a bird's wing. The woman touched her gently and told her that she had a serious illness. The traveler accompanied the woman to her tribe, where she received immediate treatment and became healed. After a few weeks, she was able to leave . . . but a huge storm frightened her, and led by a deer, she found shelter beneath willow branches. Walking on the next day, she approached the land of the bandits and came to a Great Wall. Not knowing how to get over or through the wall, she again felt very afraid and alone. Slowly walking along the wall and wondering what to do, she found no solution. One night, when led by the stars, feeling quite desperate, she began to pray. The act of praying helped her fall asleep and rest for many hours. Next morning, refreshed by her sleep and walking in a stream nearby, she stumbled upon . . . of all things . . . an Internet Café. Reluctant at first, she began to email her friends and family for help and did a Google search on climbing the Great Wall. Much to her surprise, her brother came up with a solution. Together with friends and family, they flew to her side where they built a huge ladder and climbed to the top with her. They lowered the ladder to the other side . . . and now they were in the land of the bandits. Again, much to their surprise, the traveler with friends and family was welcomed by the bandits. After several days and exchange of blankets and stories, they began to ask about the traveler's sister. They took her to see the queen of the bandit clan, and this was her sister. Even though the traveler was suspicious at first because, for too long, she thought she could do it all alone, she couldn't. Friends and family rejoiced in their reunion and joined in a big celebration, bandit-style.

After Suzanne had finished the exercise and taken some time to observe her triptych and writing in silence, she shared her experience:

When I sat down to start to write my story, my mind went blank. I had to force myself to begin and put the pen to the paper. But then, what you had mentioned is what began to happen. Once I started and with the outline of the hero's story somewhere in my mind, the words and sentences just seemed to lead one after the other, and it felt ok just to let it go without putting a break on anything . . . I know that I consider myself a seeker, but I have not thought about how much of the things that I would consider as obstacles may have another side to them, when becoming the hero and moving through them. It is amazing how anxiety about scary things can be so wrong and opposite of what your mind has been telling you. Looking at the images now, I feel less vulnerable seeing that the brave hero is actually always with me . . . interesting . . . will take some time to get used to.

Returning to Wonder Through Our Artful Lens

To return to the free-flowing creativity of our childhood wonder requires moving beyond our reliance on words to express what is in our minds and hearts. As children, we used drawings or other art almost daily to express ourselves and share our feelings with others. We also used our bodies and movement to create relationships with our caretakers. We smiled, we cried, or we held up our arms to be comforted. In this way, creative yet wordless communication was an inherent adaptive behavior for survival.

In revisiting our childhood wonder, I suggest a weekly practice of experimenting with different art materials. This will help you gain confidence in your art-making and begin to nurture the joy of expression. Make a creative date with yourself and write it down in your calendar. It is helpful to begin with a six-week block, or a timespan that you feel will work for you.

All our meaningful activities begin with a warm-up. Whether we are a dancer, singer, pianist, tennis player, or long-distance runner, we always start by stretching our limbs and moving our joints to wake up the synovial fluid that assists our body in maintaining strength and flexibility. Athletic activities are not the only ones that require a warm-up: physicians, scientists, actors, and writers also do warm-ups. I believe that any activity that has the potential to bring awareness, presence, meaning, and purpose to our endeavors requires a transition from one physical or mental form to another. During the warm-ups, we allow ourselves the time to detach from our external activities and move into our inner creative energy, where we reconnect with our true essence.

Below are four prompts for warm-ups that I use with students. Use the ones that best suit you. The important aspect here is to allow time for transition from other daily activities to your inner creative agency. In my own experience and that of my students, these warm-ups substantially contribute to a smooth transition into the creative process.

- *Silent Awareness:*
  Find a place that is comfortable where you can rest both feet on the floor. Close your eyes and let go of everything that does not concern you right now. Listen to the silence within and then connect to your body by bringing attention to your feet, and from there slowly up your legs, spine, chest, shoulders, neck, head, arms, hands, and fingers.

- *Breathing:*
  With eyes still closed, begin with a deep breath in and then let it out. Allow the next breath to flow in all the way down below your belly button. Continue this breathing without trying to control it, but simply be aware of noticing your breath, in and out.

- *Movement:*
  To bring your energy back into all parts of your body, stand up with slightly flexed knees. Move your body from your waist slowly from side to side with your arms hanging loose and following from right to left for a few moments. Next, shake out your wrists while bringing your arms up above your head and down a few times. Finally, bring your fingers into a fist, open them up, and stretch out all fingers together. Continue this fist opening and closing for twenty-one counts. By now, your breath and body will be like a new and oiled tool ready to embark on your creative process!

- *Letting Go:*
  This may take some time, but you will find it easier the more you practice. Imagine letting go of your external mind, past experiences, and judgment. Simply *be* where

you are now, creating new blueprints for a future path by allowing sensations, feelings, and images to come to you. Not forcing anything, but just be open and notice what may come.

The purpose of the warm-up writing prompts to start the exercise in each chapter is for you to free-associate your imagination in writing form. There is no need to share this or to think about grammatical rules. Don't look back; just keep writing until the allotted time has passed.

Then you are ready to "dive in" and see where the brush, crayon, or pencil takes you through the various exercises in each chapter. Allowing the suggested art material to lead you is like learning to play the scales on the piano. You'll begin to experience how colors, shapes, and forms coalesce into a full and coherent image. After a few weeks, you may begin to notice a new connection to your own "voice."

Exercise:
The Story of My Journey

Warm-up Writing:

Spend five minutes describing:

- Your favorite childhood story.
- An imaginary safe space.

Materials:

Paper
Pen, paints, markers, etc.

Instructions:

1. Begin this exercise by writing your own hero's story. Start with "Once upon a time." Fill a page or two and allow the story to unfold without grammatical or "realistic" corrections.
2. Draw or paint a triptych of three images that depict facing the obstacle, overcoming the obstacle, and what new paths now appear.
3. Give each drawing a title.
4. Attach the paintings on a wall where you can view them together. Allow yourself time to silently discover your fullness and "live" your story.

Exercise Reflection:

Consider what skills and wisdom you've gained that you can use to meet any future challenges and give you the confidence to explore new horizons.

I often reflect on these few lines from Mary Oliver's poem "The Journey," as they captured my own return to self and my creativity during a transition of darkness and uncertainty:

. . . the stars began to burn
through the sheets of clouds,
and there was a new voice,
which you slowly
recognized as your own,
that kept you company
as you strode deeper and deeper
into the world,
determined to do
the only thing you could do —
determined to save
the only life you could save.

Chapter Three

Reframing Creativity as Essential to Your Life

A human being would certainly not grow to be seventy or eighty years old if this longevity had no meaning for the species. The afternoon of life must have a significance of its own and cannot be merely a pitiful appendage of life's morning.

—C. G. Jung

Creativity has always been an essential part of people's lives, survival, and evolution. It is embedded in our genes. Our ancestral humans lived in close contact with nature, where everyday challenges of the external world—often life-and-death challenges—had to be creatively attended to in ways that involved all the senses. Unlike our close cousins in the animal world, we humans have no physical means of protection. If we only relied on the speed of our two legs, almost every animal could catch up with us for an easy meal. With no sharp canines, gripping claws, or protective bodily covering, it is a miracle that our species was able to survive. Creativity is what kept us alive. Our senses, together with continued experience in trial and error, helped us devise innovative solutions to protect us from a hostile environment.

The first historical evidence of visual art appeared during a phase of human development known as the Upper Paleolithic Age, which lasted from about forty thousand to ten thousand years ago. Our earliest known ancestors, however, are known to have lived more than two million years before that, during the Lower Paleolithic Age, when tools were used to feed themselves and their children, find and collect edibles, arrange a safe place to sleep, and protect themselves from predators. Ingenuity was crucial to our survival, and it's likely that the humans who were not able to think and act creatively did not survive. They likely fell prey at a faster rate than their cousins, who could foresee and plan how to stay safe and thereby extend their "creativity DNA" for generations to follow.

Creativity Leads to Communication and Expression

When did everyday humans begin to use images to communicate and capture important events with some form of creative expression to learn from and imagine their own future? Who were the first artists? It is believed by historians that the first artists were most likely shamans, religious practitioners who historians believed first appeared as early as the Paleolithic period. They were considered "magicians" who were believed to embody divine powers of inspiration. They were respected for their ability to enter the underworld and bring forth images that would both heal and inform. In modern times, the shamanistic use of images of our ancestors can be inspiration for our own healing and reflection.

Most of us are familiar with the discovery of ancient cave paintings, and how those images seem to reflect the expressions, needs, and activities of the people who created them. Detailed paintings of humans and animals going back tens of thousands of years have been found at Lascaux and Chauvet in France. Recently, animal cave paintings dating back to approximately

45,000 BC have been discovered in Indonesia. We can only speculate on the purpose of these paintings, but it's likely that the animals depicted in these ancient images have a spiritual meaning. From Paleolithic cave paintings, we now know that humans have expressed themselves graphically for various intentions. The paintings are believed to have served mystical or religious purposes in expressing the hunter's mind for a successful hunt.

Throughout the ensuing centuries, the magic and mystery of images began to be incorporated into the architecture of public buildings as well as royal castles. Think about when you visit a cathedral in a large European city, where stories of saints and martyrs decorate the walls. The belief was that these ornamental paintings could stimulate the devotion of the people, instilling them with virtues such as charity and forgiveness.

As human creatures, we evolved to use art to serve a myriad of political, social, and psychological purposes. Ellen Dissanayake, anthropological scholar and author of *What Is Art For?* and *Art and Intimacy: How the Arts Began*, confirms the three ways culture began to integrate art for communication and expression. The first is when societies adopted physical forms of art such as singing, dancing, or dramatizing. Second, an artistic approach was applied to the use of language. How written words and language became an outlet for creative expression can be found in what is believed to be the world's first novel: *The Tale of Genji*, written in eleventh-century Japan by a female writer known as Murasaki Shikibu. The first English-language novel was Daniel Defoe's *Robinson Crusoe* in 1719. Lastly, skillful crafts such as weaving, woodcarving, pottery, and even architectural decoration slowly became known as art-making. These creative activities were pleasurable experiences for the everyday person, which is what this book is all about. People began to use their own talents to make art instead of only relying on professionals for image creation.

When we first start making art for ourselves, we begin to experience glimpses of our creative joy, but the more we practice, the wider that door will open and invite us to a new and richer level of life. One thing to keep in mind on our expressive journey is that we create solely because it gives us pleasure; we may be surprised by our process, excited that we are able to visualize and enjoy our finished creation, and peaceful as our mind stills into one-pointed focus when we are fully present to our art project. Problems with our art-making only occur when we begin to take ourselves too seriously. This is where we get stuck and limit ourselves, which slowly closes the door to our creative practice. If we feel that this is happening to us, a helpful antidote may be to step back and remember how much fun we had when experimenting with art as a child. This returns us to the joy in each moment of our creative process. We get back to that lightness of spirit inherent in play and creativity.

Even though we often long to express ourselves creatively and dream about embarking on an exciting new project, we may find ourselves hesitating. We might tell ourselves that now isn't the right time, or that we're too old to start something new, or that whatever we make won't amount to anything. It's striking how naturally we seem to limit ourselves instead of taking that bold, creative leap forward and making the first move on our journey. This hesitation is, I believe, part of a natural process—I feel it myself, time and again. It seems that we are born with both a push to move forward, grow, and learn and a pull that holds us back. But when we allow ourselves to pull back, we remain stuck and we go nowhere. When we listen to that inner push, however, what we encounter may not match our expectations, even though it may be precisely what we need at that moment. In following this calling from within, we find ourselves moving forward—toward new experiences, insights, and joyful expressions.

In my first meeting with a group of people who had no or little previous art experience, I suggested experimenting with pieces of colored paper. About forty various colors, tones, and shades were laid out in a rainbow-colored snake in the middle of a table. Participants were asked to pick up five colors to begin an abstract layout. Christina, a woman in her mid-sixties, entered the room late after the other participants had picked their colors. She was elegantly dressed and outspoken, mentioning that she might have to leave early. She reluctantly picked up the five colors but could not bring herself to begin any layout. Feeling a sense of frustration when I asked the participants to title their image, Christina wrote down her title as "Spite."

However, after further weekly meetings, Christina became more enthusiastic. Looking forward to each class, she combined her images with words, which allowed her strong personality to come forward as she was able to express feelings that she might have otherwise held back, both for herself and in communication with others.

At our last meeting, the participants arranged their weekly images on the wall and designed their own "art exhibit." Viewing their images this way and taking some time to contemplate their creative development, they were asked to put a title to a personal emotion that was brought forward. Christina named her exhibit *Transition*, and in a tentative but also excited voice, she told me:

> *I know that I did not really want to be here the first day we met, but looking at these images now, I don't know if I have the words for what I have done. That is why I put the title* Transition *on my exhibit. Before I came here, I would never have thought that I could make anything creative. But when we were trying different materials and allowing some time for the process in my images, it was as if I was invited to parts of me that I know, but they are also*

hidden. The creative circle has helped me to become more energetic and to be able to feel and act on new initiatives. After the loss of my husband, I became very despondent. But I enjoyed coming to the circle, one of the best things I have done for myself this year. It all came as a surprise . . . even when I did not know what to do, and that fit me perfectly.

As we age, it is not unusual to look back on our lives and consider how we behaved and what beliefs motivated us. How has my life made a difference, if not for others, then at least for myself? What have I learned from my mistakes and from my successes? At midlife, our thoughts about who we are as humans begin to shift. When we transition to a new road map and creative quest at this stage, we are slowly getting used to hearing a new voice from within. As is often the case with something new, even if it is how we use our own voice, we may find that we are not always immediately accepting of this shift. That is the time when our recognition and patience in letting go of conditioned judgments and regrets can be our most important learning opportunities and allies on our journey.

Tapping into Our Mythological Past and Present

One of the foremost scholars on the importance of myth in human cultures is Joseph Campbell. Through his books such as *The Hero with a Thousand Faces* and *The Power of Myth*, Campbell introduces the concept of the hero's journey that is the basis of myths throughout cultures and across centuries. According to Campbell in *Myths to Live By*, many of our everyday experiences can be traced to our mythological past. Although myth in our everyday language is often associated with a belief or idea that is false, an imagination of supernatural beings, or incredible and fantastic folktales. People often think of myth in derogatory terms, something that's in opposition to our conditioned belief in science and facts. The root of the word *myth* comes from the Greek word *mythos*, which means "word, speech, tale, or story." This is a more inspiring and guiding use of the word. It is believed that the purpose of myths throughout history was to entertain people with adventures, fantastic beings, and ingenious strategies on the part of the hero, while also imparting wisdom and eternal truths.

The use of myths has been with us as far back as we have been able to determine the earliest birth of our species. Myths were a way to learn from ancestors, bringing a layer of magic and wonder to awaken us and to expand our view of the world. Throughout history, mythology has been the foundation for how we human beings behaved, thought, survived, and met death. Unfortunately, it is no longer mythology that consciously binds us together as humans. Scientific facts and technological tools have usurped our mythical icons as our primary way of transmitting knowledge. Today, most of us are only vaguely familiar with mythology or the importance of a higher cosmic order that guided our ancestors.

Myths, whether we are conscious of them or not, can help us see the meaningfulness of the life wisdom we have gathered by midlife, that the afternoon of our lives has significant meaning, as suggested by C. G. Jung's quote at the beginning of this chapter. Our morning and midday of life is devoted to learning to fit into our families, our society, and our culture. In a science- and technology-driven world, we learn to survive by creating for ourselves a skill that is considered a contribution to our society. We build a home, we buy the latest car model, we travel to exotic tourist resorts. Our interests lie in the news of the day and the problems of the hour, while the state of our spirit is rarely on our agenda.

Having lived our lives in pursuit of these external goals, when we face midlife and its inevitable transitions, we are unsure how to process the change and successfully continue our growth. We have all heard of the midlife crisis, which some of us experience firsthand, or we may know of friends and family members where this transition is apparent. Jung suggests that this time is not an obstacle to be avoided but a wake-up call to embark on a more meaningful and introspective learning period that may continue to develop for the rest of our lives. It takes courage and curiosity to move forward and through the transitions and callings during the various phases of our aging. Without the subconscious knowledge and interaction of myth in our daily lives, we may feel at a loss when we no longer find meaning in our activities.

Campbell believes that the loss of myth in our education and entertainment has led to the loss of signs to guide us along our way. We no longer rely on the perspective of stories from ancient times that have supported human life and civilization for millennia. We are left to work out our inner problems by ourselves. This may bring a sense of feeling both lonely and stuck.

American psychologist Rollo May, author of *The Courage to Create,* suggests that the main obstacle to reaching into our inner life is a lack of courage. Even though midlife greets us with new insights, new possibilities, new wisdom, and both psychological and spiritual phenomena, we do not always have the courage to experience this on our own. May explains our problem in moving forward is often that our own anxiety and possible new insights frighten us too much if we are to take full and personal responsibility for them. But then he goes on to say that if we look at our calling as if in a dream or listen to Socrates's philosophical maxim of "know thyself," then we may be able to be more open and forward about our truth. If we bring his thoughts to the process inherent in our own creative expressions, we may find that our imagination opens up to a wider landscape where our heart is speaking louder than our mind.

In other words, there is a helping hand to guide us by tapping into our subconscious and through the stories we create, which allow us to experience some mystery and magic. When embarking on our creative journey, it may take some practice to let go of our rational mind and stay open to our inherent instincts and to the voice of our soul.

In the 1990s, I held an open art studio in a hospital in a busy section of upper Manhattan in New York City. It was attended by people who had been or still were patients at the hospital, and some with various addictions. Barry, a man in his late forties, often came to the open studio. Sometimes he only wanted to have a chat; other times he would sit down and start to use some of the art materials that were set out on a large table at one end of the room. Barry was addicted to heroin. He had been treated with both maintenance therapy (switching to a substitute such as methadone) and detox (gradual withdrawal of the toxic substance). But neither of the treatments had been helpful for Barry, who had learned to live and function with his addiction.

If you met Barry in the street or at the salon where he worked, his "mask" was that of a relatively healthy man, well dressed, somewhat thin, and with a strong gait. Barry had, in his earlier and nonaddictive life, been a very successful hairdresser and stylist with his own beauty salon. Once the addiction took control of his life, he was no longer able to maintain his salon, which he had to sell. But since then, he maintained his profession as a hairdresser while working every day in a beauty salon that belonged to a friend and former colleague. Barry made enough money during his working hours to be able to pay for his rental apartment, his bills and food, and the costly addiction to heroin. He had accepted himself as a drug user and was able to maintain his working profession. Barry felt in control of his two worlds, one where he had control of his income and paying bills, and the other, which was the drug world that primarily involved obtaining and using heroin. He discussed his long-standing interest in biology, neuroscience, the workings of the brain, and how heroin ultimately affected his body. He was an avid reader of scientific articles where heroin addiction was the primary subject. He wanted to know.

Barry was deeply aware of his vulnerability due to his heroin addiction. Putting a hand over his heart, he told me, "I know where I am now, and I know that I will not live into old age, but before I die, I want to know who is in here!"

After Barry had finished his collage at one of our meetings, he felt that he had come closer to answering his own question. At the center of his collage were two stylized golden-yellow figures, resembling abstract human forms, reaching out toward each other. Their hands nearly touch, evoking the imagery of neural synapses transmitting signals. These figures are layered over jagged purple shapes, which may symbolize the complexity of the brain's structure, the mind's inner workings, or the emotional landscapes that shape our interactions.

Above the figures, bold blue curved lines and triangular shapes resemble synaptic waves or energy transmissions, reinforcing the theme of communication, whether neurological, emotional, or interpersonal. The symmetrical design suggests balance and reciprocity, emphasizing the essential connections between individuals, neurons, or ideas.

Beneath the artwork, the handwritten phrase I WILL MEET YOU AT THE SYNAPSE underscores the intent of the piece—a poetic expression of shared understanding, meeting points in thought and emotion, or the intricate dance of neural firing that allows us to experience consciousness and connection. Overall, Barry's piece conveys an uplifting and thought-provoking message about how our minds and relationships are built on the invisible yet powerful synapses that bridge gaps, whether in our nervous system or in human experience.

Barry explained his reaction to what he created:

> *When I look at this picture, I feel like I am more than two people. I live at least two different lives, but I know that they constantly meet in my biological body. Sometimes I feel like I imagine how life would have been for the Greek mythological gods and goddesses, some half human and half god. As in this image, I feel that I am barely holding on to the ground that I walk every day, but at the same time, I look pretty happy being transparent. Maybe in the end, that is what or who I am—a mystery.*

There comes a time when many of us would like to know who we are walking with on our journey. To know our own truth takes a great deal of both courage and contemplative inclination.

Rather than seeking to find the meaning of our life, which can seem like both an overwhelming and elusive quest, perhaps there is something else we are looking for. Maybe it is the longing to genuinely know who is inside of us, in the words of Barry, and to feel that we live our life fully with abandon and truth.

Exercise:
Exploring the Myths of Our Ancestors

Warm-up Writing:

Spend five minutes considering:

- One of your ancestors wrote you a postcard. What does it say?

Exercise:

Flags throughout history and cultures have primarily been used as identification and communication of who we are and where we come from. In this exercise, design a mythological flag that connects you to the beliefs or ambitions influenced by your ancestors.

Materials:

Colored pieces of paper

Instructions:

1. Cut, draw, or create shapes to become symbols on your flag that represent the beliefs or ambitions of your ancestors (e.g., a moon, trees, birds, hats, flowers, etc.).
2. On a neutral or colored background, arrange the pieces to depict your ancestral clan.
3. Use a glue stick to adhere the colored pieces to the background.
4. Attach your flag to a wall in front of you, where you imagine that your flag can be viewed and recognized as your ancestral signature.

Exercise Reflection:

Write a story about what the symbols in your flag represent—your beliefs, your mysteries, your own self. We are used to icons representing an object, a wordless direction, or an emotional expression. While each icon only contains its own limited meaning, symbols go further. Symbols connect us on a deeper level to our past and future, and to the mystery in which we live without limitations. Contemplate the differences between the icon and the symbol that you may have used in your flag.

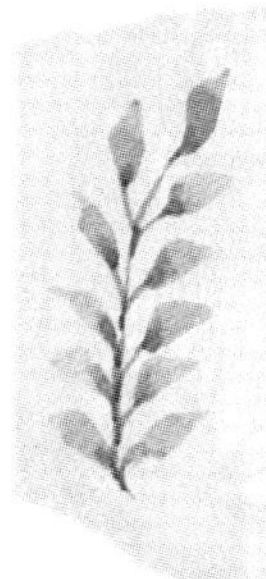

Chapter Four

Cultivating Your Artful Lens

Let the beauty we love be what we do.
There are hundreds of ways to kneel
and kiss the ground.

—Rumi

Our souls are naturally hungry for beauty. The primary way of cultivating our artful lens is to become aware of our need to find beauty in the world. We often look for beauty in art, music, landscapes, gardening, clothes, friendships, and ourselves. When we do not see the beauty around us, the beauty cannot possibly be present as an affirmation of our own inner beauty.

Some of us lead our lives in search of that missing, ephemeral sense of beauty that lies within us. A call for the affirmation of beauty in our lives can be witnessed in the millions of selfies sent around the world each day, calling out for a "like" and to be seen for who we believe we are and what we are experiencing. Even though a selfie, a photographic image, is but an external representation of ourselves and perceived differently by each viewer's individual conditioning and history, we are easily caught in the web of our own conjecture of how the selfie represents us.

Being present to genuine beauty means that we can feel the inner joy that beauty brings, permeating our physical self and leading to a sense of fulfillment and meaning. As Irish poet and author John O'Donohue suggests, beauty awakens something deep within us—it reveals what is usually unseen through visible form. To truly receive this gift, we are called to develop a more mindful and receptive way of engaging with the world.

At midlife, we may feel that the beauty of life that brought us joy in our youth is slipping away. My experience is that there is no better guide to finding beauty again than reconnecting to the kinds of play we knew as children. It is in the universal and ageless act of play that we release our imagination. Not only does playing facilitate emotional health and a sense of joy, but it is also in playing that we are able to communicate the beauty that spontaneously comes forward from the depth of our soul, our inner voice. As children, playing was the most natural way of *being*; it became a way of communicating long before we were able to use language. A three-year-old may draw a picture to show their love to a parent. Or toddlers re-enact playing house, serving each other "tea," or tucking each other into bed. Long before they know words such as *like*, *love*, or *care*, they are "playmaking" to express their feelings and joy.

When we embark on the second half of our life, we've often lost the belief that play is natural. But we can trust that its presence is still underneath layers upon layers of life experiences that have accumulated impressions and memories since childhood. In cultivating our artful lens, we are supported in the meeting of our old friend "play" again. The rejoicing brought forward by this meeting can show us the way to unexpected surprises and spontaneous expressions. The door to our creative potential is once again open when we release our imagination and become the child in us that is forever present but not always recognized as our true Self. Play in midlife, which can be fun, relaxing, and eye-opening, will lead us on our new creative path to magic, mystery, and continued curiosity.

We may find that the midlife road is paved with chaos. Both familiar and new barriers are blocking our journey forward. But with play and imagination in our emotional toolbox, we can embrace chaos as a necessary part of our growth that brings new beauty, meaning, and insight to our inner landscape.

A participant in one of my workshops had never created any art during his working life. After early retirement, he felt a need to get to know his creative side to continue to learn about himself. Here is what he said after a day of making self-portraits. "So many things came out when doing my self-portrait, things that I hadn't been thinking about. I became so much more when making these paintings . . . I was so focused on what I was doing, it was as if time stood still. Looking at it now, I can see new dimensions of myself, that are yet familiar . . . as if doors have been opened to a new and more me."

Being Present to Beauty

We find and are fed by beauty in the places where the truth—pretty or hard—is revealed in physical form.

—Oriah Mountain Dreamer

As the saying goes, "Beauty is in the eye of the beholder." To find beauty, the beholder must be fully present and willing to connect to that awareness within themselves to appreciate and enjoy the beauty that is all around them. We have all experienced the feeling of being low and lacking the energy to connect with the beauty that could lift our moods. We recognize we may no longer have the level of energy that we enjoyed in our twenties or thirties. Getting dressed in the morning, there are no clothes that feel right. The clothes we thought looked beautiful and had a lovely texture when they were bought a few weeks ago, now do not look so good after all. Thinking of breakfast is beyond comprehension; well, maybe a cup of coffee will do to maintain the morning ritual.

Walking out the door, we may not be present to the birds' morning chirps or the fresh, clean air. Maybe we suddenly realize we are late for work, and with great haste, rush along to catch the bus or train. Finding a seat, we catch our breath and with a stone face look straight ahead or down at our trusted smartphone, like the rest of the passengers. We may not be expecting any incoming message, but clutching the smartphone has become an ingrained habit to calm our breathing for a moment. But wait. The person sitting next to us is seemingly relaxed, looking around with a smile on their face. What is wrong with this person? Or rather, what is right? Shifting the thoughts to our own morning experience, we wonder what we could possibly have to smile about.

Yes, beauty is all around us, but we often don't feel or see it. The interesting thing about beauty is that it is always there. Beauty does not care if anybody ever notices, or what sort of weather conditions may bring out its full potential. When we approach each day using our artful lens, we will slowly notice a shift in how we view our everyday surroundings, making each moment a more visually powerful experience. Our mind may not always be consciously aware of our surroundings, but on a subconscious level, the memory of our experiences lies dormant until a time and opportunity trigger a moment of beauty and bring it to the surface.

Walter, a participant in one of my workshops, was considering retiring after many years as an owner of an art gallery. Art and creativity were something that had always surrounded him during working hours. Now he mentioned a feeling of both relief and sadness in meeting this new transition in his life. But inspired by a childhood memory, he painted a tree that had special meaning to him. After the weekend workshop and feeling more settled in his decision to embark on a new path in his life, he mentioned while looking at his painting:

> *When I began to make this drawing of an old oak tree, memories from my childhood came flowing back to me. I could suddenly remember how excited and at the same time comfortable and at home I used to feel when I climbed a favorite oak tree as a child. I often played by myself, and it is the same with this tree. It is on top of a hill . . . sort of by itself, like me . . . the other trees are farther away. It is the kind of tree that you want to go to. It is a tree to be protected by or to climb up into. When I was a kid, I used to climb up into the tree and be totally covered by the foliage. From a distance, it looks like all foliage, but when you climb up and into it, there is this whole open space of branches going in all different directions . . . it is very comfortable. Looking at this tree now brings back the nurturing and protective feeling it gave me, as if enfolding and welcoming me in again.*

There will be times when we truly feel that we *are* present and aware of the beauty around us and that it will leave a deep impression on us. With time and new experiences that bring varied filters to our perception of those impressions, the feeling that we enjoyed in the moment may be brought to a new and different level of joy and insight when we practice using our artful lens by engaging in creative activities. In capturing that wordless sense of beauty in a tangible form, such as a drawing, painting, or piece of music, it will hold the gift of that memorable experience. The image may be made in haste while the memory is still fresh, such as writing down your dream before it leaves your consciousness after awakening. But once you have made that first image, it may be an inroad to further creative imagination.

"Be where your feet are" is another expression that can help us find presence in the moment we are in. In this way, we also connect to our body while sensing the important connection to grounding, both internally and externally. When we become the witness of our silent monologue with a sense of curiosity and surprise, we begin to notice a shift in awareness. After a while, we feel more clearly that our feet are truly connected to our own grounded truth, and we will see that beauty is indeed all around us.

When I was a student in textile design at Pratt Institute in New York, I worked every Tuesday night and weekends at the Metropolitan Museum of Art in Manhattan. It was a great privilege to be able to walk through the halls on those weekend mornings before the museum opened and see the most exquisite artwork without any crowds blocking the view. I would always stand in front of at least one painting for some time without thinking about what the artist could have meant, or how the color palette and composition combined to form the full image. Instead, I let go of thought and relaxed my body while tuning in to the energy inherent in the painting in front of me.

Viewing artwork in this way becomes a deeply personal connection to the time and vibration of the energy imbued by the artist at the time of execution of the painting. Most of us, including myself, cannot walk through a museum each morning, but we can still be present to the beauty of a new bud on our flowering tree or a newly potted plant in our window, a bird in flight, or the full moon shining through a shroud of clouds.

There is an exercise that many of you may have done in middle school or later, where you start with a drawing of one shape, and then as you move your pencil around the shape, it slowly morphs into something else. The purpose of this free-flowing exercise is not to make any presumption of what the last image would be. The process of emerging images seems to take on a life of its own. Every single object that exists in our world has a life of its own, although we may not always see it as such. To connect to it, we need to shift our actions from how we normally go through our days, rushing to meet our appointments and finish our errands, and stop for a moment to become aware of ourselves in our surroundings.

Here's an exercise to help uncover that underlying life around you. Pick an object that you consider unattractive, or even plain ugly, then sit with this piece and observe it in silence. Slowly, as you keep looking, you will see deeper into this object, and after some time your sense of the object as being "ugly" will morph into a new and different perception.

Embracing Play as Our Way

It is in playing, and perhaps only in playing,
that we are free to be creative.

—D. W. Winnicott

We all have different responses to art materials and a blank piece of paper, from enthusiasm to fear and resistance. The only place to start the creative process is precisely where we are and to keep making choices to experience how the art slowly takes shape and moves in often unexpected ways. When we notice resistance and critical judgment, we accept that this is part of the process. We leave those self-limiting notions behind us as we move further and deeper into our creative journey.

Take a moment to wonder where that fear and judgment come from, then make the choice to let go of that fear and continue the process with a lighter feeling. As in life, making art is a process; we add one color after another, making one mark after another. We make adjustments; we throw something out and start again. Like children learning to walk, we stumble and fall, but we get up again and again, determined to follow our path ahead and to meet this new world. We understand that the tools we choose for art-making have a life of their own. They may not always follow what we have in mind or what our untrained movements of brush, pen, or markers are trying to leave behind on paper or canvas. After some time, we will sense what resonates more readily with us and with what creative material we feel most at home.

Here is where play becomes a necessity. In D. W. Winnicott's seminal book *Playing and Reality* (1971), he relates children's playing to concentration in adults. The child does not usually have the extensive vocabulary or command of language it takes to convey the infinite varieties of play. However, as grown-ups, we may find it uncomfortable or not serious enough to relate to our creative art-making as play. As adults, we consider our "play" to be more focused on creating something functional, such as a beautiful bouquet of flowers or setting an elegant table for a meal.

Play is one of the most joyful times in our childhood. But play is also necessary as adults, bringing a deeper meaning throughout our lives. In *Merriam-Webster*, there are more than eighty variations of meaning attributed to the word *play*. I find the most fitting description of play as the "freedom or scope of activity: full play of the mind." As serious adults, we tend to remove ourselves from the joy and exhilaration inherent in childhood and play. We find it challenging to remove our self-imposed barriers of rejecting play as an inappropriate activity. When we rekindle the freedom to enjoy our inherent wild spark of creativity, we bring forth our unique voice through art. However, we do not have to fear that we will lose our stronghold of control by resorting to play. With experimentation, we discover that we can have both control and play, which often makes the experience more real and accepting.

You can discover more about a person in
an hour of play than in a year of conversation.

—Plato

By inviting play into our lives on a consistent basis, we slowly start to separate ourselves from fear and our need to control the art material to comply with what we have in mind for our image. We begin to accept that the image we create is always valuable, even if we spend too much time on making it. In that push and pull of wanting and not wanting, we learn to *stay with it* to find the inspiration that lies in wait as we develop our artful lens on life. After a short time, we begin to play with the art material. We let the paint or crayon move over the paper with a life of its own. Allowing the medium to introduce itself, allowing it to speak its own language, we continue the creative path ahead with a sense of curiosity and surprise.

Playing, as we know from observing children and remembering our own childhoods, is inherently exciting while at the same time risky and precarious. Even though some anxiety may be felt when we plan in our mind what our artwork involves in our everyday creative activities, there is an underlying sense of satisfaction . . . an essential satisfaction that we are invited to be wholly who we are, and to be heard and seen foremost by ourselves. Yes, creative activities are often an intensely private journey, one that you may not readily share with others until you have had the time to absorb what your created image is conveying from your own personal perspective. A caveat here is to be aware of the inescapable fact that anyone who has the opportunity to observe your private artwork may share their well-meaning personal perspectives. I always enjoy and am grateful for the remarks of those observing my own artwork or photographs. This is a valuable learning experience and a widening of our own perspective, as long as we remain aware that those sentiments, for now, belong to somebody else.

Rhonda had recently retired from her job to take care of her husband, who had been diagnosed with early-onset Alzheimer's disease. As the only caregiver, she mentioned that she felt isolated and withdrawn from her previous friends and colleagues and that she was no longer able to share her current situation and emotional worries. Rhonda signed up for one of my art-making seminars to try to create a new space for herself and later discussed her experience:

> *By looking at their images, I felt as though I was learning their story, feeling their emotions, and creating meaning for myself. I was really impressed by the ease and discussion our images could prompt about deep issues. We got to know each other in the group in a whole different way than when we just meet and talk. When we are together in a group of creativity and paint, I feel that after a while, you also give more . . . you can contribute something to the collective.*

Releasing Your Imagination

Imagination will often carry us to worlds that never were. But without it we go nowhere.

—Carl Sagan

We use the word *imagination* in our everyday language. We say such things as "Can you imagine so-and-so just took place?" or "Imagine what you could do if you won the top prize in the lottery" or "Imagine what it would be like to be stranded on a desert island." But when we are asked to draw a picture from our imagination, we often come to a screeching halt! Why? As Carl Sagan, author, American astronomer, and planetary scientist, said above, imagination may carry us to worlds that never were. Some of us may experience this imaginary and unknown reality as frightening and unreachable. Maybe we keep our distance from it, sensing that it might make us feel insecure and less important. Yet, when we are gently introduced to that inherent imagination in all of us, we will meet a wide landscape of worlds that are filled with a blending of compassion, humor, and insight that will assist us on our way *home*.

The term *imagination* comes from the Latin verb *imaginari*, meaning "to picture oneself." This root definition of the term indicates the self-reflective property of imagination, emphasizing it as a private sphere. Here, I will use imagination as the power to create in our own mind before transference to the chosen medium. The transition from carrying imagination as an abstract idea in our mind and to manifest that imagination in a piece of artwork may seem daunting for many of us. The problem is that we tend to want to rush to see the result. But this leaves no room for the unexpected turns in the creative journey. What happened to the beginning, the process, and shift in our mindset? It is in the process of coming to the surface that our artwork makes sense to us; the images rest on a foundation that often is not verbalized. When we step aside and mainly serve as the conduit for that voice that is waiting to emerge, it will be recognized anew based on current perception and wisdom.

Every time we look at an image, we open ourselves to our imagination. No matter how limited, blocked, or preconceived our conceptions, we cannot help but make meaning of what we see in front of us. One definition of *imagination* in *Merriam-Webster* is "the act or power of forming a mental image of something not present to the senses or never before wholly perceived in reality." It may be argued that nothing can be wholly experienced in its own sense of reality, as we all will come to our imagination from personal projections. Even though the experience in our imagination may never seem true to anybody else but ourselves, it is the most important ingredient to inspire us on our journey, or we will go nowhere.

Exercise:
Expanding My Imaginary Artful Lens

Warm-up Writing:

Spend five minutes listing:

- Beautiful images, real or imaginary, that come to mind.
- Plays, movies, or books that you enjoyed as a child, adolescent, or adult.

Let's allow our artful lens to lead our imaginations into a deeper and more meaningful space to view our own and others' artwork.

Materials:

Use your own image, such as a photograph or small framed piece of art in your house, or find an image from a magazine or book that catches your attention.

Instructions:

Write your responses to these three prompts about the image:

Form in your mind a quick initial response or impression of the image.

- Take more time to see what is in the image.
- Allow yourself to "walk into" the picture. Imagine that the image is looking back at you as much as you are observing it, while creating a two-way relationship.
- Make a note of what this image is about for you, privately.

Exercise Reflection:

Compare your initial response to your second response. Notice if or how the initial impression is different. What strikes you? Is it disturbing, peaceful, spiritual? Did your emotions change about the image the more time you spent with it?

Here is an example of a student's artful lens on this image that shows how we can free the imagination to go deeper with an image:

Roberto Márquez, *Galileo's Riddle*

Initial Responses:

1. The image felt "haunting; there was a great depth of fear."

2. After looking at the image longer, the student began to wonder, *What would it feel like to be on a different planet,*

knowing nothing but what I could see in front of me and what I feel underneath me? With the warm coloring of the earth and the sparse growth of vegetation, the landscape looks more friendly than haunting. However, what is lurking above looks more ominous and unpredictable. The warm and light colors in the foreground contrast with the dark and cool clouds in the background, creating a fast and deep vista to a never-ending feeling of space. We are, of course, equally convinced that we know as much about the universe today as people were convinced of their knowledge when the Earth used to be flat. Looking at this picture is like looking at the stars. It takes me away from the energy drain of everyday mundane worries and confusions but carries me to a place of a larger space of universal importance and beingness.

3. Were your two impressions the same? The student wrote, *No, I don't feel any fear now but more of an interest and wanting to know more. The person in the picture sitting in a relaxed and open position, who does not seem to feel any fear or confusion, gives the landscape a much friendlier feeling than if nobody had been there. I think that I am that person.*

Chapter Five

Finding Inspiration in Nature

Often forgotten is the fact that we are a part of nature. Our need to connect with it is innate. When it's lost, we suffer. When it's restored, we thrive.

—Tom Stoner, Co-Founder, Nature Sacred

Over the centuries, people began to distance themselves from their ancestors' instinctual affinity for land. Many of us have lost our deep knowledge of what it means to be human beings as part of the wild nature. Our current urban and suburban lifestyles rarely include a deeper opening to nature and our inherent wildness. We are constantly reminded of natural disasters, such as fires and floods, around the world, which creates even greater fears of venturing into the wild. The emotional consequences of this anxiety-provoking information can be noted in the exponential growth of nervousness, worries, depression, and other psychological difficulties.

It is not possible to know how our ancestors felt and reacted to their own experiences of war, pandemics, fires, floods, and other natural challenges. But what we do know is that they had a closer alliance with Earth and nature. Many lived in rural villages and supported themselves by their own or nearby harvest. They had knowledge of the various seasons, the movements of animals, and the rotations of the sun and other planets.

Our increasing reliance on technology means that many of us are spending even less time outdoors today than we did only a couple of decades ago. Many have not experienced much nature even as children. Nature may seem intimidating and even frightening to some people when going on a wilderness hike unless they are protected by a group leader. We may become aware of a lingering abstract sense of fear without knowing exactly what to be afraid of. There is mounting evidence from many research studies that nature provides benefits for both physical and psychological human well-being. Scientists who study the benefits of various environments on humans have found that not only green spaces but also blue spaces, such as marine and freshwater, are beneficial and can help us thrive.

Most of us today live in populated areas with private or public green spaces filled with elements of nature such as trees, bushes, flowers, and water. We are grateful to the landscape architects who know the importance of parks when designing our urban and suburban environments. One of the most famous of these landscape architects, Frederick Law Olmsted, designed New York City's Central Park in the 1850s and created many large urban park systems along the East Coast as well as the campuses of Stanford University and the University of Chicago. It was his emphasis on the psychological effects of scenery that informed his design principles. Olmsted maintained that the experience of scenery was visual and wrote of the relation of sight to the well-being of the whole person: Whereas landscapes provide "a relief from the rigidity and confinement and protrusion of art of the ordinary conditions of the city," they are able "to refresh and delight the eye and through the eye, the mind and the spirit."

Many of us who live in larger cities will probably agree with Olmsted's words. Just look at how busy parks around the world become during the day and especially during the weekends. There is a deep-seated wordless need for our bodies and minds to connect to our natural Self by walking among green trees and plants and beside moving water. Most of us have been fortunate to feel the relaxation and rejuvenation from walking on a wooden path, from gazing at a flowing river, or maybe just from sitting on a park bench and in stillness taking in the abundance of variations in our environment. Even when we are not able to go for walks in nature, we can connect to the healing power of a potted plant on our windowsill or a newly cut bouquet of flowers. When my aging aunt Ruthel of ninety-eight years was no longer able to go outside for a walk, or even to sit in a wheelchair for a short distance, it was the cut flowers that visitors brought that gave her immense pleasure and joy.

Nature Supports Us During Transitions

Nature has the power to heal and inspire us in potent ways. This was recognized by Tom and Kitty Stoner, who felt a need to make the benefits of nature accessible as part of daily living for all, especially when living in urban or suburban settings. After moving from rural Ohio to the urban environments of Washington and Baltimore three decades ago, the Stoners quickly observed the lack of nature in cities. They also noted a sense of restlessness and fatigue from the speed, noise, and chaos inherent in intense and modern city living. With a lifelong appreciation of nature and its healing aspect, the Stoners believed that nature is a right that should be afforded to every individual and to populations who have been hit by various traumas, disasters, and general stress.

They embarked on a six-year research project in collaboration with leading figures in social research and landscape design. Congruent with the Stoners' vision, science was showing that being in nature, even in short visits, can improve wellness in lasting and meaningful ways. In the years since they founded Nature Sacred in 1996, the Stoners' vision of green spaces has spread throughout communities in the United States. In their words, "After two plus decades of listening, learning and doing, we are more convinced than ever that nature is nothing less than essential to individual—to societal—health."

If there's one thing we know as we are reaching midlife, it's that there are always transitions, often unexpected, that we need to navigate. It has been said that the only thing in life that does not change is change itself. What we don't know, however, is how we are able to cope with those changes. How do we appraise changes that come to us? Do we see change as a challenge, disturbance, or threat? Or do we see it as an unforeseen opportunity? Maybe it is different from day to day. Like a flickering flame, our moods, interactions, and environmental influences are in constant fluid movement. It is as whimsical as the ever-changing wind, like the ripples on the ocean. That is who we are. We are nature; we are a living, breathing organism like millions of other species on this planet, and we have intelligence, which may be our biggest strength in the universe.

Another part of our strength is the ability to think and act creatively. Transitions that occur around midlife can be a source of apprehension, anxiety, and worry. How will life change after retirement? How is my health? Will I be a burden to anyone, to society, to myself? And on it goes as our mind keeps doing its job with our hardwired DNA that looks out for possible threats.

Here is where nature can be one of our foremost supporters and healers. How, you may ask, especially if nature has not been your closest companion and ally. When we open ourselves to unbounded time, to connection with our conscious awareness, and when we let go of all or any expectations, a new world of pure *being* will slowly emerge as a sensation, image, or feeling. This may take time and practice, and we may need to develop our patience in reining in our chattering mind to gently return to the voice of our surrounding natural environment. Nature can, by example, invite us to our own natural *being* as opposed to our conditioned behavior of spending our awake hours *doing*. Nature is the space where we allow ourselves to go deeper, to experience, to evolve, and to grow. As the always-present biological art form, nature invites our artful lens to connect to the essence of our expressive needs, devoid of premeditative thoughts and results. Wild nature invites us to be genuinely present, to be raw and real, no filters, no mask, and opens us to new creative expressions of our choice. Nature can be there to give us a push to express the courage that comes from the deep roots of our authentic self.

In the words of Lyn Dalebout, poet, author, and environmental educator, "The wondrous cliffs and deep abysses can bring us down some days to the bedrock of our being, sometimes with a brutality that is hard to understand. It speaks the language of physiological cellular catabolism—the breakdown of the old—and anabolism—the construction of the new."

I have lived and worked in urban settings, such as Chicago, Buffalo, and New York City. During a decade spent living in Manhattan, my apartment was located on the West Side of town, while my place of work was situated on the East Side. A bus went crosstown through Central Park in midtown. My eyes were able to see and experience trees in the park from behind the bus window. Author Peter Wohlleben (*The Hidden Life of Trees*) would call these urban trees "street kids." I smiled when I saw these beautiful street kids, as I was reminded that I also was a street kid. However, this street kid was able to move from city parks to indigenous nature, whereas trees also move but at a slower rate than we will notice in our lifetime. I learned from Wohlleben that with the climate-changing weather becoming warmer, the trees respond by sending their seeds with the wind farther north, where before they were not able to survive the harsh winters. Thereby, they are literally moving. We are fully aware of the fact that everything, maybe especially nature, changes, even though that change is not always discernible to our conscious but time-limited awareness. However, not only do your mind and body change and feel better when you are close to nature, but your imagination becomes more accepting because you see a wider world, and you become part of that world.

Being Truthful Like a Tree

There's nothing that keeps its youth,
so far as I know, but a Tree and Truth.

—Oliver Wendell Holmes,
"The Deacon's Masterpiece Or, The Wonderful"

Sharing about half of our DNA with trees, our respective interwoven relationship with them is felt as we immerse ourselves in nature. Walking through a park or the woodlands can engender a sense of renewal, wonder, and a special closeness to our own ancient roots. Many of us seem to have a special relationship to trees, or maybe to one special tree that means a great deal to us, as it did for Walter in the previous chapter. Walter mentioned climbing his favorite oak tree as a child and how that brought back comfortable memories. With the addition of the timespan since childhood, a present perspective brought a new and wider meaning to Walter's oak tree.

Using the newfound awareness in your artful lens, take a walk in nature and experience the wordless sensation as you feel drawn to a special tree, an open field, or fallen branches making their own pattern. We are drawn to the source of that encounter. Maybe we walk around the source and view it from different angles.

Consider taking a small notebook and writing down what immediately comes to mind without any conscious corrections. It is in the experience of the encounter that our creative process begins. Rollo May says that we, in that moment of encounter, become absorbed in our source: ". . . the encounter may be with an idea, an inner vision, that in turn may be led off by the brilliant colors on the palette or the inviting rough whiteness of the canvas."

Many of us are not used to walking in nature and focusing on a special encounter. We may simply enjoy going for a nature walk, listening to the peaceful stillness, while getting away from man-made noises, buildings, or events. An encounter is an experience that we cannot force. It will eventually come to us when we remain open without voluntary effort. As Jungian analyst James Hollis explains, in ancient times, such encounters—whether joyful, terrifying, or awe-inspiring—were seen as openings to the unknown. The images or sensations that emerged from them, whether tied to a divine presence, a striking event, or an overwhelming emotion, served as gateways into deeper mystery.

On most early evenings, I go for a walk in the woods with my loyal dogs. After being inside teaching or writing, I welcome the therapeutic routine of breathing the fresh air and meeting the wild nature on our walks. I try to be present for nature encounters and often bring my camera. Maybe I suddenly see something that captures my imagination; the encounter creates a connection that makes me stop to look deeper, walk around to view this object from different angles. Like a sculpture, the object has a 360-degree variation in visual experience. I only know after this process that there were no external thoughts of concern, no shift in temperature or time. There was only stillness and presence. A form of meditation or mindfulness.

This short encounter has the power to imbue us with a creative energy that gives us a sense of deeper joy to carry with us as we continue our path to greet our next encounter. It is not always that I take a picture of an encounter, but I may catch some images on my smartphone for the sake of memory or information. This is a good reminder of what I want to play with later: the colors, shapes, light, time of day, or even time of year. Sounds of whispers or music may come to your imagination. Below is an image that was taken on one of my afternoon walks, where the words I put down felt as if they wrote themselves. I was just the conduit. In the stillness of this encounter, mythological stories came forward and asked to be heard. I encourage you to make your own imaginative story from your next encounter.

For some time now on my forest walks, you have been calling me from afar. I have been trying to reach you, forcing my way towards you through undergrowth and heather. But with the darkness approaching, I have had to turn back. This day, as the sun moved towards evening, my eyes caught your glimmering form through the branches. I knew that I needed to come close to you.

I stand in total silence, letting the tension of your presence sweep over, around, and through me. With all my senses present, there you are gazing at me, as I gaze back at you. Your magic and mythical proportions engulf me. I feel as if I have no breath. My heart stands still.

Persephone, emerging from the depths of the earth to meet the light, your beauty is palpable. After two-thirds of the year in the underworld with Hades, you again emerge to embrace the season of growth and abundance, wrapped in budding tender shoots. Like golden layers of ambrosia and nectar, a shawl woven by Athena during your long absence now plays around your perfect limbs. A shawl befitting the immortal goddess that you are, in your role of harbinger of rebirth, of hope, renewal, and forever a reminder of the beauty and the diabolical, meeting the tension between birth and death.

Another spring day, walking through a wooded area, the light swept over a small tree that stood out against the solid pine trunks in the background. In my imagination, I could hear tones from *Swan Lake* by Tchaikovsky:

The principal dancer moves with grace and fluidity. Behind her in union, the standing corps de ballet praises her ephemeral presence. Does she feel . . . her own beauty?

Healing Power of Nature

Every tree and plant in the meadow seemed to be dancing, those which average eyes would see as fixed and still.

—Rumi

During the recent pandemic, Sofie was diagnosed with a life-threatening illness. Sofie was then in her late sixties, a full-time teacher, and physically active on daylong hikes in upstate New York on most weekends. After Sofie's husband died a few years earlier, she now lived by herself in an apartment close to Central Park in the middle of Manhattan. Because of the limited interactions with friends and family imposed by the pandemic, Sofie's only face-to-face contact with people (albeit behind a face mask) was with the physicians and nurses who were her caretakers during the illness. Her beloved wild nature and peaceful day hikes could no longer be reached. Sofie's treatment continued over a period of two years, and the relief was deeply felt once she had regained enough strength to walk the short distance into the nearby park. She described the encounters when sharing her photos:

> *It is difficult to explain with words the deep sense of sharing that I am now feeling when I can visit these magnificent American Elms. I have always loved the trees that I meet on my nature hikes up north and elsewhere in my travels, but now somehow there is a sense of closeness that only seems to exist in the experience, the experience of sensing the life in the elms in the same moment as I feel the life moving through me. Maybe it is extra special as I now can visit them relatively regularly and follow their change, as there is also this change in me. Somehow their changes are like my changes . . . so biologically normal and natural. The Elms are protected from extinction and saved*

by fences . . . as also I am protected . . . they lose their leaves, and their shape becomes vivid . . . and then there is growth, the yearly cycle starts anew . . . I can recognize what each tree goes through within my own being. Sitting in their presence, contemplating my dear friends, I feel renewed every time after our visit . . .

The three images that Sofie shared with me were taken across different seasons. They tell a quiet yet profound story of resilience, change, and the solace that Sofie found in a nearby park during her illness. These images speak not only of trees but of the passage of time, the cycles of life, and the enduring presence of something greater than us. The following is a brief description of Sofie's images.

- *Spring/Summer Image:* Bathed in golden light, the Elm trees stretch their branches skyward, their canopy full and thriving. The sun filters through the fresh green leaves, casting intricate patterns on the grass below. The trees stand tall and protective, their limbs twisting with an elegance shaped by time. There is a quiet warmth in this image—a feeling of strength, renewal, and vitality. For Sofie, standing amongst these trees may have felt like standing in the embrace of life itself, a reminder that growth continues, even after hardship.

- *Autumn Image:* The season begins to shift, and the Elm in the foreground now wears a mix of green and yellow leaves, some still clinging, others scattered on the ground. A black metal fence runs across the frame, creating a subtle boundary between Sofie and the tree—perhaps a reflection of the way illness can create both connection and distance from the world. This is the season of letting go, of honoring transition and change. The tree remains, but it is no longer the same as it was in summer—just as we are never the same from season to season in our own lives.

- *Winter Image:* The stark silhouette of the Elm against a pale winter sky brings a sense of quiet introspection. The branches, now bare, weave an intricate, almost calligraphic pattern, telling a story even in their emptiness. A lone bird perches on one of the highest branches, a symbol of patience, observation, and perhaps a messenger of hope. The tree, though stripped of its foliage, is not lifeless—it is merely resting, preparing for the return of spring. This image carries the weight of reflection, of endurance, of finding beauty in stillness. For Sofie, this season may have been one of surrender—an acknowledgment of nature's rhythms, of the unknown, of the necessity of both loss and renewal.

Together, these images form a visual meditation on life's unfolding. Through spring, autumn, and winter, the Elm remains—adapting, transforming, yet unwavering. For Sofie, these trees became companions, guides, and silent witnesses to her own journey. The trees do not fear the coming of winter, nor do they rush the arrival of spring. They simply exist, trust, and continue—a lesson in resilience for all who pause to notice.

Exercise: Tree of Life

Warm-up Writing:

Spend five minutes describing:

- A tree in terms of a human being.
- A time when you felt at peace in wild nature. Be specific about your emotions.

Materials:

Colored paper
Glue stick
Colored markers

Instructions:

1. Draw, cut, or paint a large bare tree in winter.
2. Cut out shapes of leaves and branches to represent people, pets, and places from various times in your life. Also, from an imaginary future.
3. Glue the tree to a large piece of paper, then glue the cut-out shapes to the tree where they belong.
4. Use colored markers to identify the shapes.
5. Give your tree a title.

Exercise Reflection:

Ponder the changing characteristics of yourself (the tree trunk) in the meanings of the different shapes. Write a paragraph for each shape. How have the shapes influenced, changed, or expanded on the growth of your trunk?

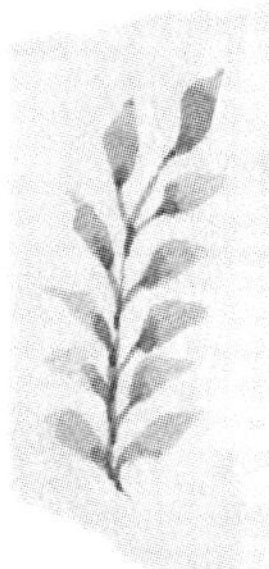

Chapter Six

Tapping into Your Senses

It is important to know that all knowledge begins with sensory perception.

—Joan M. Ericson, *Wisdom of the Senses*

It is not unusual to say or feel that we *sense* something. There is a special, maybe abstract feeling that seems to linger in our atmosphere. Even though we might not immediately have the words for what it is that weaves this tapestry of *sense* together, we are aware that it has a background of previous experiences. It could be a singular sense or a combination of senses, such as a special scent, a sound, a taste, a vision, or a recognition of connection to our body. When we use the word *sense* as in sensing that something is occurring, or sensing a special emotion, it means that all our senses are being tapped for information.

Ancestral humans lived in close contact with nature, where everyday challenges of the external world, often life-and-death challenges, had to be creatively attended to in ways that involved all their senses. Sight, sound, touch, smell, and hearing evolved so that humans could engage with the natural world. By listening to the messages from their senses, individuals used their whole bodies, breath, and muscles in their creative endeavors. We talk about our five senses, but it's likely there are more senses that inform us of our surroundings and various energy levels shared by objects in our environment.

Developmentally, throughout history, we have become drawn to what we consider aesthetically preferred sensory information. We attach a certain value to what our senses deem beautiful and uplifting, or what comes across as ugly and depressing. For example, when we see a painting with colors that have clarity and vibrance, it may indicate a feeling of freshness and ripeness. Movements that are strong, vigorous, and graceful, whether in physical sport or dances, are associated with health, control, and vitality. Although we all vary in how we see colors and how we appreciate movements and the sound vibrations produced by various instruments, there is usually a basic understanding of how and when our senses communicate a certain feeling.

Bonnie Bainbridge Cohen, author of *Sensing, Feeling, and Action*, explains that the body's ability to sense is continuously received from our skeleton, ligaments, muscles, organs, glands, brain, blood, and eyes. Even though no information is lost by the unconscious, it is the *conscious* awareness and alertness of a feeling that leads to perception and thereby our chosen action. There is a difference between sensing something and feeling something, which leads to an action, than if you simply *do* it, according to Bainbridge. Whereas our *sensing* is related to the nervous system via the myriad sense receptors alerted by both outer and inner stimuli, our *feelings* are related to our circulatory system, such as the lymphatic and cerebrospinal fluids. Our perception of the world around us thus becomes the recipient of the combined flow of both sensing and feeling.

Just think of the many movements and ritualized actions we perform every day without giving it a second thought: from brushing our teeth to getting the morning tea or coffee going, from moving our arms and legs to get them dressed, to how we put one foot in front of the other and hold on to the railing when walking down a steep staircase. Our feeling and sense of where we are in space is taken over by our unconscious awareness, for which we are immensely grateful.

Senses Inventory

Over the next week or two, jot down when you've been aware of something that triggered your senses in ways you hadn't noticed before:

- New sights
- New smells
- New sounds
- New touches
- New tastes

Which of these sensory experiences gave you joy? Brought up a happy memory? Made you want to share it with a partner or friend? Inspired you to try something new?

Arnold Mindell, a psychologist and author, wrote in *The Shaman's Body*, "After all, you own nothing but your own inner impulses." Impulses can be viewed as our physiological call to action, where our senses gather information and send it to the thalamus, a two-lobed structure at the top of the brainstem that acts as a relay station for incoming sensory data. The thalamus then forwards this information to the appropriate areas of the cerebral cortex, often referred to as the mind.

The mind processes these impulses through a combination of memories, moods, past events, desires, and learned experiences, creating a unique perception. This perception is the only thing that truly belongs to you. As the experiencer of your environment, only you can express this experience through your creative art-making. This idea relates to a presentation I attended many years ago by the renowned neuropharmacologist Candice Pert, who stated, "Your biology becomes your biography." The question we may ask ourselves is whether we are ready, able, and willing to follow our impulses to action, which may lead to change in one way or another. However, we always have the choice when we become aware of our impulses to manifest them in a creative expression of our emotions in a dance, a song, or a painting.

Our Senses Guide Transitions

Laura came to see me after she had been advised that her contribution was no longer needed at the office where she had worked for the last twenty-two years. She was at a loss for how to feel, how to be rational, and how to connect to who she really was and where her life could take her at this time in her mid-fifties. How would this shift have an impact on her relationships, both with her previous colleagues and with her own family and friends? Maybe most of all, how would she see herself and her future that was in the process of shifting?

With many confusing thoughts circling around, Laura found it relaxing to let go of her thoughts and simply use colors to fill a page with her restless energy that did not seem to find either direction or grounding. No words were needed; Laura used the touch of the paintbrush and followed the forms and colors that came to her without any conscious effort.

Here is a description of Laura's work in finding grounding and joy while creating two paintings, allowing her to release anxiety and let go of overthinking.

- For her first painting, she used watercolor to move freely across the paper, creating a continuous flow of shapes and colors. She covered the entire surface, sometimes allowing colors to overlap, other times leaving distinct color fields. The focus was on movement and spontaneity rather than planning or control.
- After completing the first painting, Laura took time to observe it carefully. She was encouraged to notice where her eyes were naturally drawn—perhaps to a specific color, shape, or movement that captured her attention. Once she identified this focal point, she outlined a small **two-inch rectangular section** around this area.
- Next, on a new sheet of paper, she recreated the **enlarged** version of the rectangle, carefully matching the colors and shapes as closely as possible to the original. Imagine using a magnifying glass to zoom in on the area that caught your attention—that's what the second painting will represent.

To complete the exercise, Laura engaged in active imagination. She gave her second painting the title *There Is an Opening* and reflected on what message it held for her. She contemplated what this small, magnified section might reveal that she had not noticed before.

Laura shared her newfound thoughts:

When I looked at the first painting, it reminded me of a large, contained fire in the springtime, so I called it Burning Flames. *Looking at the second image, the enlargement, I called it* There Is an Opening *because these words came*

> *to me when I saw that there was a small opening of light coming out of the fire behind the chaos and uncertainty in the first image. Somehow when I look at both images, I get this sense that something explosive may be needed to happen for me to let go of my previous life—that I was ready for that, and now to find the courage to go on. I will put this (second) painting up in my bedroom to remind me every morning of a new light and new possibilities!*

During the reflection of emotions from held memories, it was a comfort to Laura to see that there was an opening of light behind her perceived chaos and uncertainty. Laura discussed having observed challenging situations in her close relationships and immediate environment, which motivated her to become conscious of a way to find stability and safety in her own life, if or when she would be faced with similar difficulties. The image is a reminder of stability and purpose, as our mind has its way of shifting. Listening to the guidance from our senses may be especially helpful when we are moving through transitional changes.

When we engage in making art, what we perceive on the page is influenced by our personal histories and what we have previously experienced and therefore anticipate. As we take the time to observe and perceive what we have brought out in our artwork, our newfound discoveries bring forth a sense of joy and curiosity as we follow the impulse to move forward on our creative journey.

Getting in Touch with Your Senses

We will begin with a short warm-up of our creative imagination. As it is with all our wisdom, our creative imagination tends to dry up when it is not being used or practiced. We remind ourselves that the greatest gift that we have ever been given is the gift of imagination. Thankfully, with a little bit of warming up, our imagination will come back, and we can see it and sense it, naturally and clearly. This is an exercise of our senses that you can practice anytime. In my workshops, I read the following script out loud while the participants sit silently and comfortably with their eyes closed and listen to the prompts of their senses. We close our eyes because it allows us to move into a deeper world, a bigger world, and we are spared the impact of visual objects in our surroundings. To simply read these sentences, our mind will take over to anticipate word after word. Therefore, I suggest recording your reading on a smartphone or other device where you can close your eyes while connecting to the power of your senses.

- With our eyes closed and a big letting-go breath, we visualize a colored pen that is slowly writing your name on a whiteboard. Below your name, visualize different shapes: a triangle, a square, and then a circle. Visualize the face of somebody that you love. Then, see in front of you, from your memory, one of your favorite places in nature.
- Now, we move on to the sensation of touch, one at a time. We begin with the sensation from rough concrete as you move your hand across it. A soft feather touches your skin as you move it across your fingers, maybe along your bare arm, the side of your face. You come upon a bubbling creek, and you dip your full hand into the creek of cold water running down from the mountain. The touch from the full force of the water feels like your hand is moving along with the flow. Finally, at home, the sensation of your favorite bed sheet touching your body before you fall asleep.
- We move further to the sensation of taste. In your imagination, experience the sweet taste of your favorite ice cream or candy; the sour taste of a tart

apple, lemon, or vinegar; the salty taste of soy sauce, smoked salmon, or a special salty bag of chips; the pungent taste, often referred to as hot or spicy, such as chili pepper, ginger, or garlic; the bitter taste you may find in leafy vegetables or herbs, including spinach, cilantro, and rhubarb. Finally, imagine the astringent taste of a freshly brewed cup of coffee or tea early in the morning.

- Now, your imagination will introduce to you the fragrance of an open rose freshly brought in from the garden, the whiff from newly baked chocolate chip cookies reaching you from the kitchen, the scent of the breeze from the ocean on a warm summer's day, the pungent aroma from newly crushed leaves on a damp afternoon walk in nature.
- With your eyes still closed, imagine that somebody is calling your name. There is the sound of raindrops falling on your roof, or maybe from the inside of a cozy tent on a rainy day out in nature. Then you clearly hear the sirens from an emergency vehicle; you can hear people talking in a restaurant. Finally, back for a walk in the silence of the woods, where the birds are singing, and you notice the sound of a soft bell far in the distance.

Exercise:
My Poem Today

Warm-up Writing:

Spend five minutes listing:

- Sensory input that brings up memories.
- Feelings that come to mind when you think of a recent sound you heard.
  Example: Your cat purring (stillness) / Children laughing (joy)

Materials:

Unlined piece of paper
Lead pencil
Colored markers

Instructions:

1. When filling out your own word in the template below, begin with one of the sensations from your list above. Then follow the prompts.
2. Look through a magazine to find an image that may support your poem or draw/paint your own image.

If . . . was a color it would be . . .
It sounds like a . . .
It feels like a . . .
It tastes like . . .
The scent is like . . .
It gives me a feeling of . . .

Exercise Reflection:

In considering how greatly our senses contribute to how we view our world, how could this contribute to the art you make? If you have time, take one of the sense reflections and create a collage out of your scraps of materials.

Eric's Poem

Eric was in his late sixties and enjoyed an active lifestyle where sailing was one of his main interests. He had been a widower for over a year after losing his wife to a sudden death by pancreatic cancer. When Eric joined one of my workshops, he mentioned that he had always found it difficult to express himself in a creative way. After finishing this exercise and reading the lines from his newly crafted poem, Eric realized that tapping into his emotions evoked deeply held memories. He was grateful to connect with and discuss his memories that supported a rich lens into his life experiences, both the difficult and the enriching:

> *If affection were a color it would be blue.*
> *It sounds like a gift from God.*
> *It feels like a warm hand.*
> *It tastes like honey.*
> *The scent is like a summer's breeze.*
> *It gives me a feeling of deep joy.*

> *In my poem, I wrote that if affection were a color, it would be blue. Blue for me, it is the color of hope . . . and space, the cosmos, the possibility; it is open wind somehow—yes, the possibilities to become someone, to make something, to understand. And affection feels like a warm hand; it probably has to do with my upbringing, a faith in God. Of course, I have had both good and some not-so-good sides,*

things that I could have done better. But I have had the gift of being able to apologize when I was young and did something bad . . . somehow, I learned to do that . . . and later in life, I understood the importance of asking for forgiveness . . . something that I have tried to give to my children. Then I wrote that affection tastes like honey . . . it is a complex taste, not always sweet . . . it also contains so much . . . it is difficult to explain . . . it is an experience. You experience color if it's a painting, and it is a lot of work, as it also is to create a spoon of honey that somehow is manifested in the experience of taste. It sort of fits together those two words, affection and honey.

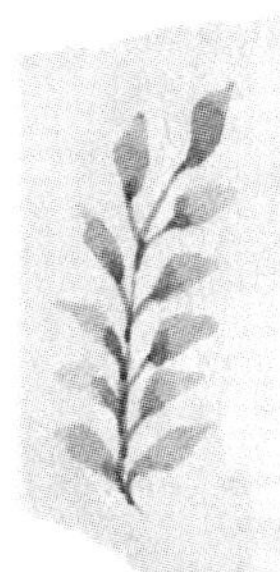

Chapter Seven

Finding Deeper Meaning

We need art to live fully and to grow healthy. Without it we are like dry husks drifting aimlessly on every ill wind, our futures are without promise and our present without grace.

—Maya Angelou, "Art for the Sake of the Soul"

Ann had retired from her career as an art teacher when she came to see me. In the transition from an engaging life with students and colleagues to her next chapter, Ann had noticed that the joy and optimism she used to feel for each new day no longer existed. She had looked forward to spending more time with her grandchildren, but even the thought of playing with them now made her tired.

In her work as a teacher, Ann had particularly enjoyed painting as a form of expression. In retirement, she began using her artwork to envision what she wanted her life to look like moving forward. Through her creative journey, she realized that she wanted to leave a legacy for her children:

I would like for them to know that there will always be challenges in life. But we go on, and my wish is that they can feel the importance of keeping a positive attitude. I learned that from my father, who was always happy despite the problems he had gone through. Now I also want to give my children a happy attitude to remember me by.

When we reach midlife, that which brings new meaning often shifts through different transition periods of obligations, in both our careers and private lives. There is a shape-shifting taking place, and we start to become aware of a silent calling from within, a calling for our own unique voice to be heard, and for an opening into endless possibilities that will bring meaning and fulfillment on our path ahead.

Expressing our emotions through art helps us chip away at the layers of self-imposed limitations that obscure the unfolding of our stories. Our stories do not disappear, although they may lie dormant for some time. Through wordless creative expression, stories may come back to us, albeit with a renewed perspective of purpose and learning. The awakening of early events and emotions may help us become aware of our unique thread of meaning that connects us to our future path. This process often brings a sense of ease when we experience the tactile movement of colors and shapes on the page. There are no rigid boundaries, no punctuations, sentences, or paragraphs to confine you, only the fluid and dynamic progression of colors, shapes, and forms as your stories and imagination are free to slowly unfold, guiding us forward with renewed clarity and inspiration.

Art-making releases a "flow" in us, as legendary psychologist Mihaly Csikszentmihalyi described in his book, *Flow: The Psychology of Optimal Experience.* He believes that our inner experiences of flow are what make a life worth living. The characteristics of experiencing flow are feeling strong, alert, in effortless control, unselfconscious, and as if we are performing at the peak of our abilities.

When we engage in a creative activity, it makes our bodies and minds more aware of our subconscious emotions. Bringing the emotions to the surface in art-making can help us act on them. When we look at our images in silence, words of emotion and wonder may come to our mind. Our newly made creative activity at midlife becomes the thread for us to act upon, an invisible thread that never left us. We may be called to take actions such as renewing an old friendship, returning to a previous hobby, committing to spending more time in nature, finding a worthy cause to volunteer for, writing a novel, or trying out for community theater. The possibilities for action that already lie within us are endless and only waiting to be brought out. This is the time to live out our individual, unique calling and often not just for ourselves, but also for the benefit of others as our truth is unfolding and shared.

In one of our exercises on making a collage, Daniel was surprised to see that most of his cut-out images were pictures of instruments. He remembered the feeling when he first heard the notes of one of the new songs by the Beatles when he was about six years old. Not being able to get the sound out of his head, he begged his parents to buy him a drum set. His well-meaning parents had other plans for their son, and Daniel eventually moved further away from his desire to pursue making music. After Daniel's recent retirement, he allowed himself to reconnect to the feeling of music going through him when looking at his collage. Acting upon that visceral sensation, it did not take long for Daniel to buy his first guitar, sign up for some lessons, and reconnect with joy to those first feelings of wonder and magic he had experienced as a child while listening to the Beatles.

Providing enough time to enter into a dialogue with ourselves encourages us to continue to learn, explore, and be surprised by what feels important now. This was recognized by some participants in a recent workshop who shared their experience:

> *Working on my image, I had a difficult time staying in the process. What would the next step be and why? I know that I also have a hard time enjoying the process of my life without constantly worrying about the future. I have an obsessive need to plan and to figure everything out. When looking at my finished image, I realized that I don't have to control every aspect of what I do to make sure it is perfect. I learned more from the joy when viewing the piece because I did not have a picture in my mind of what it should look like. From now on, when I explore future creative activities, I will work on releasing myself from controlling the outcome; it makes it so much more fun.*

At midlife, when we start to notice the shift from earlier duties and responsibilities, how and where, you may wonder, do we place our current and future duties? An unexpected and often surprising answer may come to us in the form of a wordless awareness and presence. It may be an experience that is new, unfamiliar, and yet something that provides a promise. An awakening of a promise that there is something even more meaningful that is waiting for us, where we may continue our future path of insight, healing, and new learning.

But where do we start, and how do we protect ourselves from being pulled into the allure of never-ending information and offers of exceedingly fortunate and special invitations via our social networks to everything commercial, from exotic cruises to the latest gadgets that your pet cannot live without? I know I certainly get hooked, especially when it comes to something that will profoundly improve the lives of my dogs! But on a more serious note, it is our duty to protect our priorities and desires, to be on alert to that which occupies us without thought of what may impart a sense of meaning and further growth. If we stop only for a short moment, but for as long as it takes to bring us down into silence and stillness, we will notice an inner knowing of what may bring us closer to that which we consider meaningful and worthwhile of our time.

Art Helps Us Determine Our Priorities

One of the most important and maybe the most difficult lessons in life is to learn that less is more. Yes, you have heard this before. We are ingrained gatherers and collectors of both material and immaterial belongings. However, the weight of our belongings increases their toll on us around midlife. This is a practical as well as an emotional weight that is in dire need of being lightened. Midlife is the perfect time for cleaning our closets, both from within and without. There are many positive changes as we grow older, and one of them is the relative ease and relief around our process of prioritizing. We have learned how to prioritize the use of our time on activities that benefit us energetically, while at the same time shrinking our to-do list and even leaving some empty space for rest and recovery.

Here is where our artful lens comes in to open a world where experience and imagination are invited to come forward. This invitation may only be noticed in the stillness and presence of our being as we give ourselves a short time of relaxation before proceeding with our creative activity. There will always be a dialogue between our mind and heart, and with our conscious awareness of this process while being creatively engaged, we will remember our intentions and favor our heart and spirit. The creative act of opening ourselves to our emotions during this stage of life can guide our decisions on how to prioritize our time.

In his research on creativity and aging, Gene Cohen, professor of psychiatry and the first head of the Center on Aging at the National Institute of Mental Health, identified the benefit to individuals who can engage in continued learning through creative activities with an open mind and heart. The result is that these creative activities uncover the cumulative experience of emotional, physical, and social memories and contribute to a personal and optimal experience for the event or object at hand. Cohen's research is an affirmation of what many of us already know but often do not encounter. We may not think of engaging in creative activities or be offered the opportunity to ride on the wave of what is already covertly waiting within body and mind to become an overtly tangible expression of our emotions. Studies have shown that active engagement in the art-making process at midlife evokes further curiosity and a willingness to go deeper into self-discovery. When we find the courage to connect to the rich and wide source of our inner emotions, they will be our deeply trusted source and guide on our personal journey of expressive communication.

Reconnecting to What Matters

As we age, our tendency is not to think about our everyday activities actively. We are moving into more automatic behavior—we forget where we put our glasses, or we walk into a room to get something and then forget what it is that we are looking for—while a six-year-old has continuous and present experience of their environment. But in our developmental aging, we also become more of who we were in our younger years. We allow ourselves to be more playful and open as we were as children.

In reawakening our creative and artful lens at midlife, it is important to have a focused, alert awareness of our surroundings. What does it look like? Be curious. Become an adventurer in your own environment. Notice what you see in front of you or listen to, while being open to sensory information that brings meaning to everyday experiences. This is also a way of becoming still and finding room within yourself that brings appreciation for the endless variations in your experience that your artful lens helps in guiding.

Something as simple as your smartphone (available, easy, and an immediate inroad that may spark further curiosity) will assist in seeing new ways of being. Next time you go for a walk in your village or city, or maybe just around your home, designate your smartphone to be the artful lens with which to view colors. Take five or more pictures while focusing on the color only, as much as possible, not the full item or its environment. Create an album on your smartphone where you will move all your images from these exercises for ease of later recall. After you have finished this exercise, you will become more attuned to and in harmony with your environment.

Reclaiming Our Authentic Voice

Around midlife, we may find ourselves losing meaning because we have left our primary career, our children are grown, either we or our friends have moved to new cities, and we may find ourselves in a new space. To continue making meaning for ourselves takes time, silence, patience, and the complete absence of negative judgments. We awaken to the belief that we still have the energy it takes to find something meaningful to contribute to the world, and to ourselves. We awaken to the belief that there is a story inside us that tries to unfold while bringing meaning, purpose, and wisdom to our future path.

In our earlier life, for many of us, it was the voices of others that were our priority . . . the voices of parents and siblings, of teachers and classmates, of employers and cohorts, of a spouse, partners, and children. Yes, the list can be long when we give ourselves time and silence to contemplate the voices that have brought us to the present state in our midlife era of meaningful transitions. In the beginning, you may just notice a blip of awareness into this shift before it disappears. But then you know; you have experienced this feeling, if only for a millisecond, and you begin to bring it back again, little by little. In prioritizing our own voice, we are not engaging in an act of focused ego selfishness. We are moving to a deeper and more conscious level of awareness. This is not a sign that we will neglect our continued support of family, friends, or events that bring us meaning. On the contrary, with an opening to the essence of our own authentic voice, the shared experience trickling out into our environment will be sensed, felt, and appreciated by those who matter the most.

You might be asking, How do I find the thread that will lead me back to my authentic inner voice? What makes this challenging for some of us is that we want to be liked, we want to be included, and we worry that by not speaking but simply feeling that unique depth in us, we will separate and be alone. But our own voice is precisely what we are looking for on our creative path. When we understand where the origin of the barrier to our own voice comes from (that of other voices inculcated and memorized in our mind), we can let go of the limitations, lift the bar, and open ourselves to the joy and experience of our own voice and calling.

One of the best ways to find our voice is through play. This is where we let go of all analytical judgments. There are no goals, no audience, and nobody to satisfy. You are the one and only explorer on this path toward your authentic voice. To embrace play, we become like children. We start small, without expectations. The following is an exercise in using your body in big expressive movements, letting your heart lead the way, while remembering your childlike ways.

- Put an apron on. Bring out large sheets of paper on a table or floor.
- Make large sweeping movements with charcoal or water-based acrylic paint (smaller paint sets available online or at any art supply store).
- Imagine a shape or form, a tree, or stick figures draped in flowing fabric, or anything else that comes to heart.
- Experiment further by listening to various music of your liking while painting. New paper and painting for each mood of music. Play, play, play. And remember, you are having fun, and this is just the beginning!
- When you are finished, write down five to six words that express how you felt making your images—e.g., Bold? Brave? Sensitive? Sweet? Kind? Thoughtful? Or other words that come to you. Now, imagine how you can use your voice this way in the world.

Art Helps Us Stay Optimistic

Does an optimistic outlook on life work? In the field of positive psychology over the last forty years, thousands of researchers have been trying to find out why this may be the case. How strong is the power of positive thinking? James Maddox, University Professor Emeritus and Senior Scholar, Center for the Advancement of Well-Being at George Mason University, author of numerous publications on well-being and life satisfaction, answers this relatively simple but expansive question by saying, "The truth is that believing that you can accomplish what you want to accomplish is one of the most important ingredients—perhaps *the* most important ingredient—in the recipe for success."

The very little blue engine looked up and saw the tears in the dolls' eyes. And she thought of the good little boys and girls on the other side of the unsurpassable looking mountain who would not have any toys or good food unless she helped. Then, moving forward, she said, "I think I can, I think I can, I think I can.

—Watty Piper, *The Little Engine That Could*

Albert Einstein is credited as having said: "If you want your children to be intelligent, read them fairy tales. If you want them to be even smarter, read them more fairy tales." As children, stories that were read to us were real. We became empathetic with the protagonist, whether a person, an animal, or a little blue engine. The animation of emotion and power of possibility began to form a certain thought pattern in our mind that contributed to later beliefs and determination in a voice that says: *I can*. During our younger adult years, many of us had a rather clear picture of what we wanted to accomplish. We had set certain goals and timelines. There may have been some blips along the road, but we bounced back, convinced that we could achieve our goal if we only stayed focused and engaged.

Moving into midlife and retirement, our goals begin to shift. We want more than our previous achievements offered. We want to learn, and we want to know that we are living fully and with abandon. But how? Our earlier certainty that we could accomplish anything that we put our mind to, according to Maddox, begins to waver. The road no longer seems so clear or self-evident during our time of midlife transitions.

"If not now, when?" are words that I have heard from participants who attend my workshops as we begin to discuss our goals. Many have no previous art experience, but creativity has been in the back of their minds as something to take up "later." It becomes very easy to create nothing but procrastination and roadblocks to our creative and artistic selves. An ingrained fear that we are not going to be good enough. We will be disappointed. We will waste our time. The excuses can be many, as you may recognize in reading these lines.

Melinda had been an accomplished textile designer during her earlier years. Her career, however, came to a halt when, in her forties, she married her second husband. The new pressure on Melinda as the wife of a well-known composer with a great deal of travel and entertainment left little time for her own creative joy. After her husband suffered several strokes in his late sixties and became incapacitated, Melinda was the constant caretaker during the last ten years of his life. While Melinda was working through the grief of losing her beloved, she also had to attend to financial complications due to her husband's unfinished business arrangements. This resulted in years of uncertainties and legal conundrums. Melinda was brought into a time of despair, loneliness, and sorrow.

Even so, Melinda was able to dig herself out of what seemed like a never-ending dark abyss. After a few years of feeling as if she were lost at sea with no ground to stand on, she began to pick up on her earlier skill as a designer. Melinda's creative soul became once again her cherished and steadfast companion that supported her on her way forward to the next chapter of her journey. The important part here to remember for all of us is that we, each and every one of us, have an inside space that will never leave us and is always ready and waiting to be recognized, to be heard, and to be lived. Melinda took up painting again to express her emotions. She did not feel that she had words enough to fully bring forth what was brewing, and sometimes boiling, inside of her. One of her images was a large 18-by-24-inch painting of a tree in various colors, which she had titled *Tree of Fire*. The following is a brief description of her painting.

Tree of Fire depicts a single strong tree standing against a dynamic and emotionally charged background. The tree's trunk is painted in warm golden and earthy tones, with streaks of yellow, orange, and hints of purple, giving it a sense of vitality and movement. The branches extend outward, forming a full canopy of dense foliage, rendered in dark browns, deep greens, and fiery oranges. The leaves appear to be in motion, as if caught in a swirling wind or flickering like flames.

The background is painted in an interplay of colors, suggesting a landscape alive with energy. The upper portion of the painting is a deep green, providing contrast to the glowing warmth of the tree's crown. The lower half is a dramatic field of red, orange, and dark brown, resembling fire, autumn leaves, or even scorched earth. The brushstrokes in this section are bold, layered, and expressive, enhancing the sense of movement and transformation.

The base of the painting transitions into dark, almost black streaks, which could represent rich, fertile soil or the remnants of something burning away to make space for renewal. The contrast between the glowing reds and oranges against the dark lower ground suggests themes of destruction and regeneration, power, and resilience. Melinda titled her painting *Tree of Fire*, which tells the story of the essence of the image. The tree does not appear to be consumed by flames but rather embodies fire itself—standing strong, rooted, and alive amidst intensity, symbolizing strength, transformation, and endurance in the face of change.

In earlier chapters of this book, there have been discussions on the power of symbolism in our everyday lives, how we interpret them, their emotional impact, and how we live with them. Here, both the tree and fire might hold a powerful and almost mythic presence. The following symbolic interpretations may not necessarily be how Melinda experienced them while painting, but they may serve as a gateway to deepen your insight of connecting to symbolism in your own creative artwork.

Fire can have conflicting symbolic associations of transformative power. While it consumes, warms, and illuminates, it can also bring pain and death. The most striking element in Melinda's painting is the sense of fire-like energy radiating from the tree. Fire is a force of destruction, but it also clears space for new growth. In this context, the tree may symbolize an individual who has endured hardship, change, or even loss, yet stands unshaken, transformed by the experience. It reflects inner strength, rebirth, and the power to emerge from life's trials with a renewed sense of purpose.

The tree as a symbol of life, stability, and growth: Trees are universal symbols of life, grounding, and endurance. In this painting, the tree remains firmly rooted, suggesting a deep connection to one's inner strength and foundation, even amidst a chaotic or fiery environment. The vibrant canopy, with its mix of greens, oranges, and browns, suggests a season of change—perhaps autumn, which often represents letting go, transition, and the natural cycles of life.

Overall, Melinda's painting holds a message of strength, resilience, and the beauty of transformation. It tells a story of a being who does not fear fire but embodies it, standing rooted and thriving within change rather than being consumed by it. Whether seen as a metaphor for personal growth, emotional endurance, or creative passion, *Tree of Fire* is a powerful symbol of embracing life's challenges and emerging stronger. And this is what happened for Melinda when she, a few months later after her tree painting, decided to weave the image in a tapestry. She wanted to know more and to fully feel the tactile sense of what the painting might hold for her. The following is a description of her 2-by-3-foot tapestry.

The tapestry beautifully preserves the essence of the painting while bringing a new textural, tactile depth to the image. The greens and dark tones remain rich and layered, forming the grounding presence of the tree. The fiery oranges and reds intensify toward the right side, seeming to burn, flicker, and shift as if the fire is woven into the fabric itself. The texture of the fibers enhances the sense of movement—unlike the smooth strokes of paint, the woven threads carry weight and structure, allowing the weaver to feel every transition, every burning ember, every rooted space with her own hands. The right edge of the tapestry, where the deep reds and blacks interlace, suggests a meeting of destruction and transformation—a liminal space where one thing becomes another. The colors do not simply burn out; they merge into new possibilities. There is something both wild and deeply controlled in this woven fire, as if the weaver is harnessing its power through her craft, her presence, and her healing process.

Having been a weaver of tapestries myself for many years, Melinda's journey resonated extra deeply with me. The process of moving from a painting, a drawing, or a thought to another medium that might lead you to further insight can be both surprising, uplifting, and enlightening. Maybe you will find how that first spark of your creative exploration will call you into a medium that is close to your heart, such as a song, a dance, or a piece of music.

As in all creative endeavors, there is a therapeutic power also in weaving. An energetic power of weaving is found not only in tapestries, but also in weaving yardage, blankets, or other both decorative and functional textiles. Weaving is inherently meditative and grounding. The repetitive movement—the pulling of the threads, the shifting of tension, the merging of colors—mirrors the process of emotional integration. Unlike painting, which can be more immediate and expressive, weaving requires patience, rhythm, and an ongoing dialogue with the material itself. This slow, intentional engagement likely helped Melinda process her emotions at a deeper, more embodied level.

By weaving her pain, anxiety, and transformation into this tapestry, Melinda did not erase the fire—she gave it form, gave it space, and found a way to hold it without being consumed by it. This is the essence of deep healing, not avoiding or escaping emotions but engaging with them in a way that allows for renewal and integration. This further speaks to art as a living process—not just something we make, but something that shapes and remakes us in return. Melinda wrote of her journey:

> *The burning tree was very important to me when I made it. It was the heat of anger that I felt in my body after my husband died and left in a way that was very hurtful. After my husband died, I was devastated in so many ways. First that I felt that he left me after his stroke and then withdrew into himself, while becoming increasingly aggressive towards me. Yes, I know now that it was not a rational feeling, but at the time, I was overwhelmed with emotions. After thirty years of marriage, where we had been the best of friends with each other, at least that is how I felt, but in the end, I felt that our wonderful years together ended in a state of bitterness and discord. But when I finally brought out my paint, it was a relief for me to be able to put all that anger on paper. I no longer had to carry this devastating emotion inside of me. It is hard to explain, but it was as if I was purging out a toxic substance that had been brewing inside of me, and now, for the first time, I could see it on the paper. But when I looked at my painting, it did not look angry or diabolical; it had vibrance, life, and renewal. I was surprised. I no longer felt as alone, it was more a feeling of curiosity. What is going on? Where am I going with this? At that moment, I had no words for what I was feeling, only a deep sense of some sort of relief, a recognition of a trusted friend.*

Weeks and months moved on, and after more than a year of looking at the painting that I had hung in my living room, I felt that I wanted to know more. As a previous textile designer, I decided to make a tapestry of the painting. I wanted to touch it and to feel its movements through my hands. Then something happened in that tactile activity. The translation into a tapestry that I could feel, touch, and manipulate into its true form began to speak to me on an even deeper level than what I had experienced in the painting. Again, I don't have the words for how the painting/tapestry became so deeply close to me, like the best companion and guide from inside . . . it is a mystery, and I am so very grateful that I have finally become close to this beautiful mystery that will always be with me and knowing that I will never be alone again. I have mystery, and that makes me feel very comfortable. I never thought I would be comfortable with not knowing, but now, I would not want it any other way.

We are explorers, we keep learning, we keep observing, and we never lose our sense of longing for a wordless feeling of fulfillment. At the same time, we long for the soul that has been with us all along and which distinguishes us from others. We are born to evolve; we are natural beings who constantly change, grow, and expand our vision. We don't have to be designers to bring out our artful vision of emotions on paper or in another medium. Our artful lens is evolving on par with us and will continue to be our true and trusted ally on our path forward and onward to that which speaks to us with a voice of hope, excitement, and joy.

There is joy in our experience of becoming more and more familiar with picking up ideas, art materials, and inspiration that will help put our emotions and thoughts on paper, canvas, or any other material that will surprise us by suddenly falling into our hands. Maybe something we pick up in our garden, from a walk on the beach, on a flea market, or at a garage sale will be what inspires us. We become daring, using materials in ways that we may never have thought of before, and notice the sensation of how they feel in our hands. The tactile sense of working with tapestry somehow brought Melinda closer to her emotions. We remind ourselves how touch may be one of our most precious forms of sensory information.

Jungian psychologist James Hillman, in the search for character and calling, proposed the Acorn Theory, suggesting that each person bears a unique essence that already existed within us at birth and asks to be lived. In other words, Hillman holds that we are not a process or a development, but that we are that essential image behind all our experiences and changes as we move further on our chronological scale. Looking backward, we may recognize certain traits or senses that call to us more than others. We still carry them within us, through childhood, through youth, adolescence, and onward. It is easy to believe that we are what we see in the mirror in the morning as we are getting ourselves ready for the day. How easy it is to lose touch with our soul's journey. Maybe it has to do with the fact that in our current time and society, our soul is not on the agenda in the way it has been through millennia and sacred traditions throughout the world as we know it.

I encourage you in the following exercise to reach out to the inner voice that is always with you, no matter what you go through and how your physical body and mental mind shift and change every day. As Picasso is known to have said: "I don't develop; I am."

Exercise:
Once upon a Time: Past, Present, Future

Warm-up Writing:

Spend ten minutes finishing a paragraph that begins:

- "When my train ride reached its destination, I . . ."
- "The first time that I met a wild animal, I . . ."

Spend no more than thirty minutes finishing this exercise.

Materials:

Drawing paper (12 x 18 inches)
Watercolors or colored pencils

Instructions:

1. *Past:* Draw images or use colors and symbols to represent past memories.
2. *Present:* Draw an image that brings meaning to where you are now, as in today.
3. *Future:* Draw a fantasy image of what you see in the near and/or far future.
4. Move away from your drawing, observe it in silence, and notice what you experience without any premeditated thoughts or judgment.
5. Spend ten minutes writing about your reflection of the dialogue with your images.

Exercise Reflection:

The aim of this exercise is to engage in a dialogue with your artwork that will enhance what you envision as meaningful. Engaging in a dialogue with your artwork opens the door to a deeper connection with your image, allowing you to become more aware of its evolving meaning as part of an ongoing process of communication. Make a note of what may be carried by the line or thread that moves through your images.

Chapter Eight

Meeting the World with Wonder

When one's thoughts are released to roam through the lonely spaces of the universe on a moonless night, they can be shared with a child even if you don't know the name of a single star. You can still drink in the beauty and wonder of what you see.

—Rachel Carson

I met Jim a few years after he left his job as a photo editor for a major New York newspaper. He was in his late forties when he began to accept that it would not be possible to continue with the work he was doing without serious implications for his health and overall well-being. The job had taken over his life, including creating complications with family. After two decades of maintaining his dream position, Jim began to feel a sense of disconnection from his job. He felt that he was losing his ability to care for the quality of the images coming through his office. It seemed that all he had the capacity for was going to work and coming home to go to sleep. There was no energy left over to play with or to enjoy his two children. As he explained:

As much as I loved my job, all the excitement, the speed, the best thing that I could do for myself was to leave my job. I did not know what to do, where to go; all I knew was that it was imminent for me to change my lifestyle. With no job, I could no longer afford to live in Manhattan. Fortunately, for me and my young family, I still had connections with my old school in a small town in upstate New York. There was an opening; the school needed a teacher in biology, which had been my major in college.

Moving away from the stress, the noise, and the 24/7 deadlines of my job, and landing on a quiet street surrounded by nature was a necessary and lifesaving transition. What I did not know then, but what slowly came back to me, was my love for nature and for photography. My early voice for creative photography as a teenager was lost when I began working as a photo editor of other photographers' work. Images became an objective judging of what best suited a sensational or last-minute important story for the newspaper.

But now, after my return to my own photography and being inspired by the wonder I experience in nature, there seems to be a new creative and unexpected adventure every day. This close contact and relationship with the wonder and presence of the living world in nature have brought me to a way of life that I could not even have imagined when I was in the throes of a hectic professional way of life.

After a discussion with his general practitioner, Jim came to realize that he was experiencing burnout. Although this is not a medical diagnosis, it is more than just normal anxiety, lack of concentration, and decreased performance. Burnout can create a high degree of irritability, procrastination, and being overwhelmed by even small requests. Some often stop their basic routines of self-care and daily habits of maintaining a healthy manner of living.

We have all been in periods of stress and exhaustion where we take on more than we rationally can manage with the quality that we demand of ourselves. We feel overwhelmed by our to-do list, and the backlog of important projects to attend to is steadily increasing.

If burnout has not affected us personally, most of us have family members, friends, or cohorts with persistent workplace stress or other emotional situations. Some occupations are naturally more vulnerable to the effects of burnout than others, and some people and cultures are more prone to emotional and physical depletion due to unmanageable stressors over a long period.

According to a recent Work and Well-being Survey by the American Psychological Association (2021) of more than 1,500 US adult workers, 79 percent had experienced work-related stress in the month before the survey. While burnout continues to be a health issue that medical professionals and social psychologists are paying attention to, there is a lack of understanding on how to prevent this syndrome.

Wonder was suggested as a tool for fending off burnout in a recent conference on narrative medicine, a field that was pioneered by Dr. Rita Charon at Columbia University in the early 2000s. Charon believes telling our stories in a medium of our choice, whether written, painted, sung, or danced, allows us to connect to the dynamic range of emotions that we carry with us. Emotions such as awe and wonder often help us move through difficult times and contribute to both mental and physical health and well-being. In fact, American authors and social psychologists Dacher Keltner and Jonathan Haidt suggest that awe-inducing events may be one of the fastest and most powerful methods of personal change and growth (2003). The potential power of awe to provide emotional strength is something that is often overlooked at midlife.

Jim was able to transition from his stressful New York lifestyle and job position to reach a place where the wonder and awe-evoking moments of the vastness of nature were available to him daily. Nature, with its ever-present wonder and mystery, has the potential to awaken a peaceful, rewarding, and meaningful existence in all of us. This state of stillness might not be felt from a walk in the park, or even from a weeklong excursion into the wilderness. Nevertheless, it may encourage a slight opening of a door to endless possibilities of joy and awareness. And once you get your foot into that enchanting door that is letting light through, you will want to open it all the way.

Accessing Wonder

What is in the mystery of wonder? Why does wonder matter in my life? The word *wonder* has different meanings. We might wonder what the weather will be like in the morning so we will know how to dress when getting ready for a hike up the mountains or going out for a picnic. This association with wonder is commonly referred to as "passive wonder" and implies a search for knowledge. There is no involvement of mystery or existential musings.

But when wonder matters deeply in our lives and is the focus of our creative growth, it reflects an *active*, contemplative, and curious engagement with the world. To experience the emotions of wonder does not mean that we need to reach out for something extraordinary and elusive. When we shift our heart and mind to new possibilities, the experience of wonder will come to us. It may come when we least expect it. And often not in the way we might have imagined. Sometimes it depends on where we are in life, our environmental circumstances, and how trusting we are of our awareness and truth.

Wonder might come to you when looking up at the moon in a special moment when you feel extra connected to the vastness and power of nature, or when you listen to a piece of music, or when you read a beautiful piece of poetry that resonates with you on a deeper level. Some may see this as a spiritual experience. Others may find that the most magical and wondrous moment in life is to be present at the birth of a child. The wonders that I have experienced from the kindness of strangers have more than once brought me to tears. Other physical sensations of wonder may be that of goosebumps or a tingling along the spine. Genuine experiences of wonder will not be forgotten but will leave you with a wider and deeper curiosity of what is there for you to fully experience.

Active and contemplative wonder brings us to an opening into mystery. In the quote by Rachel Carson at the opening of this chapter, she links wonder, meaning, and mystery. Wonder does not end in doubt but is the awakening of the mysterious and inconceivable. We live and develop in the wonder of the unknown. Every day upon awakening we all have another twenty-four hours of time until the next wakening call. Time is democratic. It is the one thing that we all share equally. We may have plans, wishes, rituals, or routines for how to utilize our time. But the mystery is that each minute may hold something different and unexpected to meet us. That is the beauty of the unknown.

We continually renew ourselves in many ways at midlife when we realize that transitions bring new opportunities. How should we spend our time? How do we fill our days? How do we restore our souls? We continue to build on our process of experiences throughout life. No matter what age we are, we can always begin anew, with a fresh tabula rasa to reframe our world in accordance with our creative and artful lens. The goal is exploring the freedom of how to *be* in the world, how to meet our days with new eyes and new beginnings. The shadow side of freedom is when we limit ourselves to repetitive behavior and developmental stagnation. Yet, we are born to evolve; even in the darkest moments, there is an energy within us that is always at work to bring forth our truth and deep self-affirmation on our creative journey.

Fears Might Steal Our Wonder

There's one thing that keeps us from feeling wonder at midlife, and that is persistent and underlying fears. Fear of losing our health, both physical and mental. Fear of running out of money. Fear of losing our jobs and not knowing how to fill our time. Fear for our children's safety. Fear of not being able to take care of ourselves. Fear of being alone. Fear is ubiquitous, especially at midlife.

We often get triggered by an event or someone's words, leading us to a place of previous fear or anxiety. A feeling that we no longer need but that lingers in our mind as an old imprint waiting to be deleted. Instead of taking the "easy" road of denial or suppression, it is important for our well-being that we become aware of the underlying energy-draining emotion inherent in fear. We all know our fears, and we all have them, and the fear surrounding our instinct for survival can be useful in rare moments of danger. But we have to be vigilant to conquer the fears that drain our energy, that make us tired and lose our joy and motivation. This is the time to wake up to what no longer serves us and remove the vexing worries before they linger and become chronic. Yes, it takes time to remove a long-held fear, but the awareness of what energy this fear is connected to may be helpful. We can then consciously redirect this energy to that which feeds our joy and creative soul. Our willingness to try new things and to embrace the emotions of wonder and awe will help us release fears no longer suitable to our joyous and enriching midlife transition.

Exercise: Finding Wonder in Textures

We receive tactile information about the world around us through touch every second of the day. But we rarely contemplate the wonder found in this sensory information.

Use your smartphone to take pictures of ten or more textures in your surroundings at home or while you are going about your day. Experiment with capturing textures in extreme close-up to dramatize their beauty. Look for unusual shapes, patterns, forms, and colors that are either man-made or something you will find in nature. As you are taking these images, delight in the *texture*'s information to your senses. Narrow down your selection to six images. Write a sentence or a paragraph about each texture, whether it is warm, cool, sharp, soft, silky, rough, spongy, crisp, etc. Here are six images of textures from my nature walks:

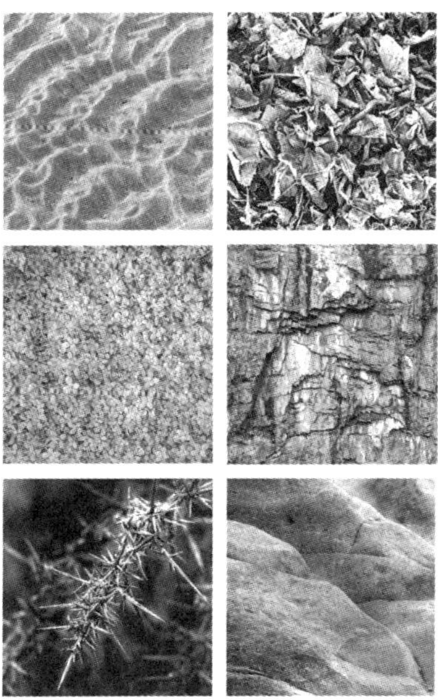

Contemplate your experience of the sense of awe and wonder of touch in your images, as if you had never seen them before. Imagine knowing that you would never touch them again. In the words of Rachel Carson, "Reflection supports us in the values of preserving and strengthening this sense of awe and wonder—the recognition of something beyond the boundaries of human existence."

Below is an image I took while walking the beach during low tide. Nature is our foremost teacher of wonder, and the flowing designs created from the ocean's ebb and flow teach us that we can move in ever-widening circles like the sand in the ocean.

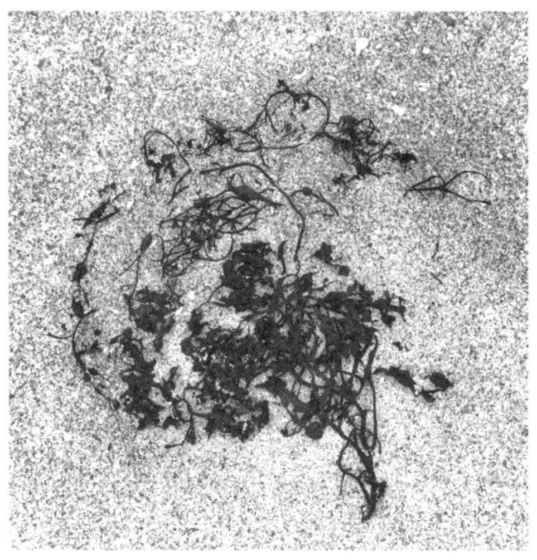

Our Daily Wonders Lead Us Forward

. . . I circle around God, around that primordial tower.
I have been circling for thousands of years,
and I still don't know: am I a falcon,
a storm, or a great song?

—Rainer Maria Rilke, translated by Anita Barrows and Joanna Macy

The German poet and author Rainer Maria Rilke lived a great part of his life in the magic, the wonder, and the mystery. In his poems, the absence of something is more mysterious and hopeful than anything experienced in presence. His imagination expanded endlessly into wonder, which can introduce us all to the dynamic growth of mystery. Rilke expresses the wonder in relationships, from the minuscule to the vast, that he found in nature: "Oh how I believe in it, in life. Not that which makes up our time, but that other, the life of little things, the life of animals and of the great plains." In *Letter to a Young Poet* (1954), Rilke expresses that turning inward through our creative development is most crucial in our process forward. It's only through contemplation that our voice is found.

Every day is a new opportunity for accepting our wondrous and mysterious life, if we only get out of the way of our conditioned thoughts, fears, and conjectured premonitions of what is to come. We have discussed the importance of staying in the process when engaging in anything creative. It is in the process that we evolve, grow, and learn, where we meet the unexpected and experience the opening of doors to endless possibilities. The only expectation of our creative development is that we connect with joy, curiosity, and wisdom.

Exercise: Wonder in Nature

During one workshop, I led the participants on an early morning walk before the dew had lifted. My prompt was to make a quick sketch or take a photo to assist in seeing deeper into our environment. One of the participants returned filled with enthusiasm as she told us: "First, I did not find anything that drew my attention. But once I decided to be brave enough to get down on my knees and get closer to the ground, it was as if I could not stop seeing. A whole new world of activities that immediately sparked my imagination and wonder at the mystery that surrounds me every day! I don't ever want to miss this adventure again."

With the mindset of play and flow, see where this experiment takes you. There is no judgment, just a sense of curiosity as if unlocking doors without knowing what may meet you on the other side. Our eyes have a life of their own, and when we experiment by following their cue, a new world may open for us.

- Bring your choice of camera or drawing pad, go out in nature, and when something captures your attention, go there! You don't have to know its name or what it is that you see, or what it is that you feel, but the inner call for your attention is enough to pick up the key and unlock that door to wonder.
- After spending some time in stillness and connecting to your image, write down a dozen words that sparked your imagination. The deepest and most meaningful emotional experience is that which is being evoked in the moment and presence of your lived relationship with your image.

- When you come back from your walk, write a short fictional story based on your image and the words that came to you while in the field or forest.

Trusting the Mystery Inherent in the Process

How often have we heard the three words "trust the process"? Maybe so often that we let it go as just another cliché with an abstract meaning that does not apply, or words that leave us in the dark. But what is the action that lies behind the word *process*, and how does it apply to us at midlife in our everyday connections? While it is a challenge to recognize and get a perspective on where we fit into our life cycle going backward, it is just as challenging to grasp our future.

We have an ongoing and dynamic process of relationship with ourselves that keeps changing for as long as we live. When we use our curiosity and courage to open the doors to that which has previously been closed to our creative expression, what unfolds may be the map that we longed for in our uniquely wild and soulful expressions. The doors might first be noticed as just slightly ajar, but if we stay with the process of their movement, no matter how strong the screws have rusted and tightened around their hinges over time, once the doors are open, they will never again be closed. Think of this as a metaphor of wonder and mystery you are about to embrace. When the process of your creative sense of self expands and breathes with its own energy, you may notice a shift in a wider dialogue, not only from within but also with your environment. When asking ourselves the question of who we are, we may find the first-century sage and scholar Rabbi Hillel's question worthy of contemplation:

If I am not for myself, who will be for me?
If I am not for others, what am I?
And if not now, when?

My client Wayne was in his early fifties and had recently transitioned to a new job position where he had yet to find a grounding sense of meaningful contribution. Having dabbled in various creative projects earlier in his life, Wayne looked for an opportunity to reconnect with that side of himself. In reawakening his creative energy, Wayne hoped that he would find it easier to be more courageous and open to the new working environment in his current position.

During one of our sessions, Wayne worked on his image of chaos. His initial emotion was anxiety in response to the forms and colors he had chosen. However, when he continued working, he also became aware of a deeper perspective that emerged from the images. He had never thought of visualizing his emotions. After Wayne moved from his chaos image to his second image of stillness and inner silence, he came to rest his awareness on a large painted heart. For the first time, he was able to visually observe the pain that he still held in his own heart from losing his brother to suicide. Wayne realized a sense of relief in being able to move his anxiety (the seemingly meaningless fate and death of his brother) to an image that became a tangible metaphor of his brother.

Here is a brief description of Wayne's first painting: This is a vibrant, free-flowing composition with expressive brushstrokes and a layered, dynamic use of color. The background consists of yellow and green tones, possibly evoking sunlight coming through trees. The left contains a tree with a twisting trunk and leafy canopy, painted in earthy greens and browns. In the foreground, a red heart shape appears prominently next to the tree connected to the ground, possibly symbolizing emotions or an anchor of feeling. A bold blue knife shape sweeps across the right side at an angle, adding energy and movement, as if making something significant of crossing into another space. Scattered details like abstract lines and figures suggest movement, people, or elements of an unfolding story.

And here is a description of his second painting: The second painting is a close-up, deeply focused rendition of the heart figure from the first painting. Here, the heart is magnified and dominates the composition, painted in warm reds and browns, with swirling brushstrokes emphasizing depth and texture. This shift in focus suggests an emotional deepening, centering attention on a singular, powerful symbol for the previous composition.

When meeting Wayne a few weeks later, he enthusiastically described how he now found it easier to delegate new and creative activities in the workplace that benefited both his colleagues and the company. Whereas he previously thought that his ideas were not good enough or that they would be rejected by his coworkers—or even worse, that *he* would be rejected—reawakening the creative core from within had given him the courage to implement his ideas. Even if some colleagues did not at first agree with Wayne, he held to the creative truth that now made him feel more grounded and self-assured. He explained:

> *When I was making the images for chaos-stillness, I was just painting and putting down colors. I was not thinking; maybe it was just airing of emotions. I just let it happen . . . first there were a lot of colors, and then it began to crystallize when I was working . . . when I started to take in the chaos . . . what I have been through in life, the regrets, and the sadness, divorce, everything painful . . . and this knife came out in the painting, and the tree . . . they just appeared. But when I looked at it later, I had painted something red, and in the end it became a big heart in the second image. Then, suddenly, it hit me! I asked the person sitting next to me what date it was . . . the 14th of March, he said, the same date in 1989 when my younger brother committed suicide, by hanging himself in a tree. So, I probably think of it every day, but I was not aware*

> *that I was thinking right then. And now I am glad that I made this painting. I have never before been able to visualize the emotions of what I have in my heart . . . and I just feel so grateful! I will not forget this feeling of wonder that seems to stay with me, regardless of time.*

When we close the door on a painful emotional event in our lives, we may unintentionally allow the lingering darkness of that experience to influence our future decisions. This was evident in Wayne's creative process. He was instinctively drawn to the image of a heart, which he interpreted as an unspoken motion toward connection. This image evoked a strong emotion in him, and this highlights an important concept: Emotions can be seen as "(e)motions"—inner motion that prompts us toward deeper understanding and insight.

The heart is universally recognized as a symbol of love, emotion, and human connection. It represents not just love but also life itself—symbolizing breath, vitality, and health. The transition from the broader scene in Wayne's first painting to the magnified heart in the second painting suggests an inward journey—perhaps from external observation to personal reflection. The first painting explores an open, expressive world, while the second brings attention to a singular, intimate essence, reinforcing themes of emotional depth and self-discovery.

For many of us, embracing creativity and following our true calling requires courage—especially when we are finally ready to express feelings that have long been locked away. It's easy to fall into the habit of repeating familiar emotions day after day, rather than taking the brave leap into the unknown. But when we trust in that leap, we discover that our full potential and freedom have been there all along, waiting for us to engage.

The connection between the heart and courage is especially meaningful. According to *Merriam-Webster*, *courage* is defined as "the quality of mind or spirit that enables a person to face difficulty, pain, danger, etc., without fear; bravery." The word *courage* comes from the Middle English *corage*, derived from the Anglo-French *curage* and the Latin *cor*, meaning "heart." In Latin, *cor* signifies not just the physical heart but also the metaphorical center of courage and spirit.

Michael Meade, a scholar of mythology, recently discussed the profound link between the heart and courage on the podcast *Living Myth.* He referenced the saying, "The only heart worth having is a broken heart," a sentiment shared by numerous writers and philosophers, though its origin is unclear. Meade suggested that heartbreak and deep emotional vulnerability are pathways to greater empathy, insight, and understanding. He argued that until the heart is broken, nothing can truly enter, and little can flow out.

Because of the large blue knife painted at an angle across the first image, I will mention a few symbolic interpretations of what a knife might signify. Depending on where and when a knife may show up in your own artwork as a symbol, some of the following may apply, or else may lead you to further personal interpretations. A knife often symbolizes both literal and emotional pain. In this case, it may subconsciously reflect the deep wound left by the brother's suicide—an event that cut deeply into his life, shaping his decisions and sense of self. Just as a knife severs, trauma can create an emotional rupture that distances a person from their own creativity, confidence, and ability to engage fully in life.

Knives can also be tools of survival, used for cutting through obstacles. This could indicate a struggle to navigate life after a loss, carrying both the emotional weight of the past and a need to defend ourselves from further emotional harm. In Wayne's painting, the knife is present but stylized, perhaps unintentionally drawn (as he mentioned, "I was not thinking, maybe it was just airing of emotions"), suggesting that this is a symbol emerging from deep within his subconscious.

For some survivors of a loved one's suicide, there is often lingering guilt—questions of whether they could have prevented it, or if they missed signs. A knife, associated with self-inflicted harm, might subtly reflect the creator's inner conflict or any unspoken feelings of responsibility or regret. The shape and placement of the knife in this composition could suggest a subconscious expression of these emotions. At the same time, a knife can symbolize transformation—the ability to cut away what no longer serves us. Given that this creative process led to a breakthrough for Wayne, the presence of the knife may indicate that he was ready, even if unconsciously, to sever himself from the grip of the past and move toward acceptance. The later shift in focus to the heart suggests that, rather than being defined by trauma, he is now reconnecting with his inner core.

This movement from the dominant image of a knife (first painting) to a heart (second painting) is significant in that it suggests an important transformation. One from being emotionally "cut" by grief to fully recognizing and feeling the pain, but in a way that allows for healing. The knife no longer dominates; the heart does. This could symbolize Wayne's moving from a place of self-protection and avoidance toward vulnerability, self-awareness, and ultimately, emotional growth.

What is striking is how the healing didn't just stay within the personal realm for Wayne. It rippled outward into his professional and social life. The deep-seated fear of rejection, which had been shadowed by his brother's tragic death, seems to have loosened its grip. Creativity, once a place of hidden pain, became a source of confidence, allowing him to step into leadership and innovation. Wayne's story shares how emotional healing through art is not just about processing grief; it is about reconnecting to life in a fuller, more engaged way. His newfound self-assurance in bringing forth ideas, even amidst possible disagreement, is a powerful metaphor for creative resilience.

When we call on our creative self to support us in removing the self-imposed veils that hide the deeper meaning of our being, the opening will feel genuine and welcomed. Genuine because it comes from our own inner truth and not from the external world. What emerges from our images may evoke a sense of purpose, motivation, and wonder.

Put Wonder into Practice

One purpose of engaging in creative activities at midlife is to rediscover your core inventive self that can never be lost. It can only be expanded upon. Your geographical, biological, and social situations may change. Your goals, friendships, and beliefs come and go. But underneath the process of your new experiences and learning, your creative voice stays with you and only becomes deeper, stronger, and more vivid in its yearning to express itself.

Then why do some of us struggle to let our creative voice be heard? There are many complex reasons, but in this exercise, we focus solely on reconnecting with the innate essence of our creative expression—one that has been passed down through generations, like an ancestral "sound" echoing through time. As we listen, we may discover that our creative voice speaks in a vocabulary unfamiliar to us. Perhaps we will never fully understand it, but by embracing it with an open heart, we can gradually come to know ourselves more deeply through its unique language.

Exercise: The Wonder of Metaphors in Relationships

Warm-up Writing:

Spend five minutes listing:

- Symbols that are important to you, and why.
- Mythological and/or geographical areas where your ancestors resided thousands of years ago.

Spend thirty minutes enjoying this exercise:

Materials:

Scraps of fabrics, yarns, and ribbons
Beads, shells, and other decorative or representational items
Heavy rope

Instructions:

1. Thinking in metaphors, choose colors and textures to represent members of your clan (family, friends, soul). That is your starting point.
2. Start out with the rope as a "trunk." Think about your "family," how you feel, and what you know about each member that you will represent. Then choose a color of fabric, or texture of wool, or other scrap pieces that make you think about your members. For example, what does the color green represent when thinking about your father's ancestors? Add on pieces as you wrap them around the "trunk."

Exercise Reflection:

Maybe more around midlife than in earlier years, we begin to contemplate our relationships and how they have changed over time. Our parents, siblings, and friends may have long since died or in other ways moved out of our lives, but our relationships with them keep changing and growing because we change. We may see our parents differently now and relate to them in a way that was not possible in our earlier years. We gratefully continue to learn and sometimes be surprised at what emotions of wonder can come to us through even a relationship that ended long ago but still lingers in our minds.

Contemplate the wonder in your relationships. Write a paragraph or list words that come to you from each member on your *rope*.

As one of my workshop participants said, "This feels very personal as it extends to relationships with my own family or clan. It made me reflect and think about what I was doing—more effort than in making the collage where I just reacted to the images. I very much enjoyed this project as an emotional link when working with my family. Family to me seems to be the most accessible to my emotions, something that I already know . . . but I even found myself imagining ancestors that I have never met or seen their pictures. I tried to grasp those feelings and stay with them for as long as I worked on each member, and somehow it was as if they came alive!"

Chapter Nine

Building Resilience for Change

Keep walking, though there's no place to get to. Don't try to see through the distances. That is not for human beings. Move within. But don't move the way fear makes you move.

—Rumi

When the pandemic became an everyday challenge to deal with for many of us, our resilience to this adversity is what carried us through. For Victor, however, being the property manager of more than two hundred buildings created a level of stress and anxiety that at times seemed impossible to handle.

As an entrepreneur in his late fifties, Victor fought hard to keep the business going, but eventually, the pandemic closed many of his buildings. Not being supported by a large corporation or any other means of income, Victor knew he had to think about a major change in lifestyle. He closed his business and sold his condominium, where he'd lived for the last twenty years. Closing a business at the same time you are selling your home, filled with memories and comfort, requires a great deal of strength, resilience, and forward-looking.

Victor packed two bags with his remaining belongings and bought a ticket to Scotland, where he had some connections, but without any further plans of what he would do in the coming months or years. With no more customers or emergency calls 24/7, Victor picked back up one of his favorite activities, mountain biking, in his new environment of the Scottish Highlands. He found that not only was nature deeply healing and calming, but he now also found time to stop his bike and pause instead of rushing through the trails. In previous years, Victor's time on the trails was limited to brief openings in his work schedule. As his eyes slowly became used to seeing the surrounding beauty of nature, he began to take pictures with his smartphone. Victor later described this experience as a felt sensation, both physically and mentally, of peace and joy, when he for the first time set aside time to truly see, admire, and contemplate his own place in nature.

After more than a year of taking images, Victor decided to try putting them together in a creative journal depicting this time in his life. He taught himself how to make a book for his images and created a tangible and beautiful affirmation of how he managed to get through a most challenging transition. Nature supported his resilience and determination to make something truly worthwhile of an otherwise difficult and life-changing adjustment.

Victor eventually returned to the US, where he has found peace and a new home in a beautiful mountain area. Victor was supported through the first years of change, loneliness, anxiety, and uncertainty by a connection to hope and possibility that he had accumulated over the years as a sole proprietor of his business. There had been previous ups and downs in the economy that had greatly affected Victor's business, which he had managed to work through. But this time, with the pandemic, there was a difference, and a new sense of resilience was required. For

Victor, it was the mountains that became his solid and reliable friends in an otherwise unpredictable turn of events. For the first time in his adult life, he now had the time to spend uninterrupted days hiking the mountains and regaining a deeper relationship to himself.

Exercise: Changes You've Successfully Made

- List five experienced transitions in earlier life, when your previous *normal* became a *new normal.*
- Contemplate what, if any, feelings of resilience you brought with you to the *new normal.*
- Write a paragraph for each transition. Write slowly, taking time to express the meaning of every word. Underline a word or two that embodies your learning experience to inspire future resilience.
- Make a loose sketch of metaphors from two of your underlined words.
- Contemplate the metaphors.

Resilience Requires Flexibility

At the core of our sense of strength, courage, and well-being lies the essential elements of trust and resilience. So why do some of us bounce back from painful experiences and life-changing events more easily than others? Early resilience researchers focused on individual qualities, suggesting that resilience is partly due to the capacity for successful adaptations in circumstances normally associated with excessive mental stress (Stein, 2006). However, Stein and other researchers are now studying resilience as a *dynamic process.* In other words, our resilience is about harnessing our adaptability and self-trust that develops over time.

From the exercise above, you may have noticed how your own abilities, decisions, and intuitions continuously change and lead you to a process of increased inner wisdom that will never cease to be your supportive guide. From the creative art activities on your future path and led by your new artful lens, you will begin to see and embrace the metaphors in your artwork that speak to you on a level beyond the ordinary routines in meeting perceived challenges. Allow for and trust in your inner creative voice to build on that dynamic process when strengthening your resilience. No matter what time, age, or media of expression, we continue to build and embrace opportunities for resilience as long as we live.

The American Psychological Association (APA) Dictionary of Psychology defines *resilience* as "the process and outcome of successfully adapting to difficult or challenging life experiences, especially through mental, emotional, and behavioral flexibility and adjustment to external and internal demands." How flexible are we generally in our everyday lives? I dare say, probably not very flexible. We repeatedly stick to our routines. We are busy; it seems every minute of the day is accounted for with organized activities, and we demand ourselves to be fulfilled to the best of our capabilities. So where do we find the opening into flexibility? How do we change a system that seems to have been working so far? Or maybe it has not been working very well, but busy as we are, we don't even have the time to think about potentially upsetting and overwhelming change.

Psychologists define resilience as the process of adapting well to changes that do not necessarily involve serious health problems, tragedy, or other sources of significant stress. Yes, of course, we hope that we have built resilience against more challenging changes, but we also need to have access to our resilience for more routine changes, such as community or societal transitions that have an impact on our lifestyles. Other than in matters of physical health, how have we been supported by our resilience? Are we building on our resilience for future challenges?

Developing a Fresh Perspective

One of the many ways to boost our resilience is to surround ourselves with a freshness of perspective. At midlife, we have "seen it all," we have "heard it all," and we have a word for everything in our visionary field. We see a rope, a rock, or a rose, and we leave it at that. Our minds have other "things" to be concerned with. But in the following exercise, we don't allow ourselves to identify what it is that we see with a familiar word. Instead, we allow the eyes to follow a certain shape, a line, or a form that catches our attention. We sense the inherent energy and movement within each item that comes across our vision; we follow its movement to the point where we can sense a nearness to its energy within our own body and rhythm. Try borrowing something from nature for a while and take the time to follow its form and sense its texture more closely. Experiment with imagining that you are a small child, seeing and experiencing the object for the very first time.

Not only are we in constant change and flux, but objects around us are also equally in a state of movement, albeit with our brief encounters, we might miss the visible changes from without. Contemplate the tension in your object where one line or form moves into the next. It is in the balancing on the edge where tension and movement are felt most deeply.

Developing Your Positive Mindset Around Change

Framing a challenge in a constructive way allows us to meet changes with resilience and determination. Our appraisal of any situation is a normal process in our everyday experiences. Our thoughts at the time shape each emotion that arises, while at the same time, an emotion can be a predictor of what we are thinking. This suggests that the cognitive aspect of an emotion is part of a person's subjective interpretation of a specific event, as noted by R. S. Lazarus, distinguished scholar and professor of psychology (2006). Lazarus further held that when we appraise a situation with negatively toned emotions, variables such as harm, loss, and threat may be applied. But another type of appraisal, that of benefit, may invite a positively toned emotion. We certainly don't walk around thinking about how we appraise the situations and events we encounter. Although over the years, these earlier encounters greatly contributed to our current state of resilience.

As we transition into midlife, we are likely entering a new phase of our lives. But at the same time, we are still holding on to the "old." We will always notice that tension of needing to go forward, wanting to go forward, but also the comfort and limiting stagnation of staying the same. We are learning how to hold the tension of the push and pull. We are not completely letting go of the old ways, and we are not shying away from taking that leap of faith into the unknown. What is waiting for us may turn out to be something that we could not have imagined earlier but now is beginning to make perfect sense.

We learn and develop strategies for effectively managing our aging path. We use the felt tension and let it lead us into an expansion and widening of our creative potential. We limit our selection of activities, which gives us space to optimize the relationship to those that we care most about. This may also entail compensation for our previous routines. An example of this can be seen from interviews with eighty-year-old pianist Rubenstein. When asked how he continued to be an excellent concert pianist, Rubenstein said that he only played a few pieces (selection) but practiced them more often (optimization), using contrast in tempo to hide finger speed (compensation). Rubenstein consciously applied this approach to his music practices, which helped him continue to play at a high artistic level late in life.

Our resilience in how we adapt to changes after midlife and later stages of life can further be seen in the creative work of the contemporary painter Georgia O'Keeffe. O'Keeffe had a long career as a twentieth-century artist. She was a pioneer of Native American modern art and became known for her paintings of richly colored and often abstract flowers, bones, hills, trees, and other natural shapes that became her trademark. When

O'Keeffe's eyesight was compromised by macular degeneration in her mid-eighties, she stopped painting. But with the help of an assistant, O'Keeffe began to work in clay and was able to continue expressing herself creatively, albeit in a new medium, until the end of her life.

Exercise: Holding the Tension of Opposites

In holding the tension of opposites, we recognize that there are two different energies with varied amounts of stress that, when combined, create a third sensation/stress. When we hold the tension of opposites long enough, a surprising third way can come to us with a truly creative solution, bringing a new sense of energy and creativity to life itself. Stress is a natural and expected feature in our everyday lives. In nature as in life, one side cannot exist without the other. Without day, there would be no night, and without division, there would be no unity. You may wonder why we would need even further stress than already experienced by one "object." The reason is that by venturing beyond what you have done or met before, you now connect to further limits of your self-imposed possibilities. Yes, it is a challenge, but you will find that recognizing the inherent energy in tension will make your exploration in life more gratifying.

- Use an unlined piece of paper and make six equal vertical columns.
- List ten or more opposites in columns one and four.
- In columns two and five, write or paint a color.
- In columns three and six, write or paint a metaphor of your word.

Example:

1-Word	2-Color	3-Image	4-Opposite Word	5-Color	6-Image
Tall	Green	Tree	Short	Red	Rose
Growth	Yellow	Sun	Decay	Brown	Soil

- Contemplate the sensation of tensions as a normal event in your life experience.
- Write a short dialogue between the two opposites. What changes? What do the opposites contribute to each other?

Diana Chapman Walsh recently wrote an article about the tension of opposites (*Medium*, 2023) after the sudden loss of her husband, who sustained a fatal head injury from a fall: "They are everywhere—these polarities in life—and we grow in wisdom as we learn the patience to tolerate the uncertainties that lie beneath them, so that we can in time open to the possibilities that arise above and around them, and into which we may in time mature."

Creativity Builds Resilience

Being resilient is not necessarily a personality trait, where some are more resilient than others. And it is never too late to build on our resilience for as long as we live. Despite and even because of our challenges, we need to seek vitality, dreams, hopes, joy, and creative activities throughout our life cycles. Resilience is often named as one of the pillars of successful aging, a phrase that was first introduced by Rowe and Kahn in the late 1980s. They stated that successful aging resulting from resilience involved three main factors: (1) being free of disability or disease, (2) having high cognitive and physical abilities, and (3) interacting with others in meaningful ways.

Other researchers have found that creativity as a means to successful aging greatly contributes to resilience, personal growth, self-acceptance, and autonomy (Ryff & Heinrich, 1997). Attendees who participated in creative activities over a period of three months found that art-making contributed to imagination and well-being in two ways: that of making and that of thinking. The connecting link of the internal world of thought and imagination with the application of realizing those ideas during the creative art process brought valuable insights, a sense of accomplishment, and an expansion of the self.

Creativity as a way to cope with changes during the later stages of life is not only something engaged in by artists who have practiced their craft throughout their lifetime. Many individuals first begin to tap into their creative capabilities after age sixty-five, at the time of retirement, when they are finally free to pursue an interest that may have lain dormant during many years of active involvement in work-related situations and other responsibilities. When we eventually engage in art-making activities, we give ourselves opportunities to experience a feeling of choice and control of our chosen medium, which is one of the contributing factors to self-assertiveness and resilience that we all need on our future path.

When Julia had a life-changing fall while hiking in the mountains of the Midwest, both her hips were crushed, and she sustained several broken ribs. Julia, then in her early fifties, was an experienced outdoor adventurer on international expeditions and trekking routes. One day, when hiking alone along a familiar trek, she momentarily lost focus on her path while her eyes followed the flight of an eagle high above. She slipped on some dry rocks and lost her balance for a second, enough to bring her too close to the edge of a cliff with nothing to hold on to. The weight of her daypack and photography equipment contributed to her fall off the cliff.

Julia's four sons would sometimes join her on the local mountain hikes. When not engaging in her deep love for nature and hiking, she was a full-time nurse at a local hospital where she was used to taking care of visitors that would come in with broken bones from skiing accidents in the winter and from minor accidents hiking in the summer, or occasionally, tourists suffering from hypothermia due to getting lost and having to stay outdoors overnight.

After Julia returned home from the hospital where she had been cared for, she was no longer able to perform any of her routine duties. Neither as the caring mother of her family nor as the excellent ER nurse at the hospital. Not only was she in physical pain, but she also suffered from the immense shock of falling down a steep cliff more than fifty feet along a craggy and rocky mountainside. She did not remember much of the fall other than thinking that she would most likely die, which she could not fathom as she needed to be there for her children. She was feeling lost and fearful of what had happened. She had been on so many more arduous hikes than this one, where she fell. How would she be able to trust again that her love of nature would be there for her with the same sense of joy and play? How could she trust her body, strength, and focus?

While Julia could not find the words for her experience of the fall, words that would help her move through her pain and fear, she still needed to somehow bring out her deep sense of insecurity and vulnerability. The weight of the emotions stuck within her was too heavy to carry, and she longed to come back to her full potential as nurse, mother, and nature lover. Not that she would forget about her fall, but she sensed that there was an energy throughout the fall that was clinging to her on a deeply visceral level. It felt as if every cell of her body was still reacting to the trauma. She knew it was not only in her mind.

Since childhood, Julia had always loved painting and still enjoyed it from time to time. Feeling the need to express herself while engaging her whole body as much as possible, Julia taped a few brown wrapping papers to the wall in her home office. Simply using white and black water-based paint, she painted out the pain of her body's broken parts to express her care and appreciation, and at the same time, her frightening surprise of a great fall where her body protected her and took the brunt of the fall. When she shared a photo of her painting with me, I saw a strong and energetic painting on brown wrapping paper featuring bold, gestural black-and-white markings that created an abstract, skeletal-like composition. The expressive overlapping and layered lines form dynamic shapes that suggest organic and anatomical elements—perhaps ribs, a leg, or a foot. There is a sense of movement, as if the forms are twisting or unfolding within the space. The contrast of black and white against the brown background gives the piece a raw, visceral quality, evoking themes of structure, fragility, and transformation. The presence of intersecting lines and repeated forms creates a sense of tension and rhythm, inviting an exploration of its depth and hidden meanings.

Later, during our discussion, Julia shared her evolving insights into an experience that brought her a new level of awareness and appreciation for her body's protective nature. Each morning, many of us wake up without fully recognizing the intricate, almost mystical interplay of cells working tirelessly to provide us with energy, nourishment, and healing. But for Julia, this awareness had become deeply personal. She said:

> *As hard as it is to put into words, finding a way to move beyond the fear and uncertainty that so many climbers experience has been challenging. But through this process, I've discovered something unexpected—an immense sense*

of gratitude and wonder for how my body protected me during the fall. This realization is something I will never forget.

Now, instead of avoiding the fearful, wordless thoughts that kept returning, I feel a deeper connection to my body through this painting. Before, every reminder of the fall sent a wave of anxiety through me, and I didn't know how to process it. But now, I find that I don't need words when I look at my painting. For some reason, it makes me feel grounded and safe. I've decided to keep it here in my office, like a guiding hand from within—to help steady me as I continue my recovery and prepare for future hikes in nature.

Exercise: Building Our Shield of Resilience

Warm-up Writing:

Spend ten minutes listing:

- Animals that are important to you, and why.
- Three to five items/events that bring you fear, and what would be the opposite of this emotion.

Spend forty-five minutes on the exercise below:

Materials:

Large sheets of brown wrapping paper or canvas paper (approximately 3 x 3 feet)
Artist tempera or poster paint
Crayons

Instructions:

In this exercise, we keep in mind our tension of opposites discussed above. These will form part of our personal shield. Native American Indians used to make these shields and hang them outside their tepee. The content of the shield would tell the story of the person living in the tepee, and others would know who they were from what was painted on the shield. For example:

North	Wisdom	White	Buffalo
South	Trust	Green	Mouse
West	Look Within	Black	Bear
East	Illumination	Gold	Eagle

Contemplate what animal feels close to you, either comforting or frightening, and connect to its character. Are they caring, are they hunters, are they scavengers, etc. Each of us has a particular medicine animal.

1. Start by drawing a wide circle with a pen and string or with a straight edge.
2. Draw your design with a variety of detail and broad open spaces, with repetition of certain designs. Draw with a crayon before starting your painting.
3. When finished, find a doorway or open space where you can attach your shield and observe in silence.

Exercise Reflection:

When observing your shield, contemplate how you connect to and identify with nature, color, different directions, various seasons, and the time of day/night. Write one page or more to go with your personal shield. What do you have in your bag of resources when meeting your future self at midlife and beyond? What resilience is to be found in your shield?

Chapter Ten

Moving Through Loss

One does not become enlightened
by imagining figures of light,
but by making the darkness conscious.

—Carl Jung

With each phase of our life, there are new questions, new information, new ambitions, new losses, and a new way to meet our everyday challenges. Moving through the stages is a process in which we all participate. Upon reaching midlife, most of us have been faced with changes associated with loss, such as losing a family member, friends, our health, our marriage, a favorite pet, and even our dreams. The transitions and changes implied with loss are universal experiences, but the personal responses to these experiences are highly individual.

We are aware that loss, impermanence, and change are part of our everyday lives, and yet, our natural tendency is to resist change, especially significant change. With our unrealistic desire for stability and "sameness," we meet that tension again. The tension of desiring our normal routines and everyday expectations, while at the same time responding to and integrating new events into our lives, creates emotions that we are at a loss to fully describe for ourselves.

Changes in our emotional and private life as well as those in nature may imply a sense of impermanence. To live and to engage in a creative life, there is a recognition that the only thing that remains constant in our changing lives is that of impermanence. The way we see the world now, and the way the world is and has been, is always changing. And just because we felt, believed, or said something one day does not mean that it will be the same another day. In fact, we, as well as everything around us, are in a constant flow of change.

Encounter Impermanence

As you continue your photo exercises, allow yourself to be surprised at how often in your daily life you encounter impermanence. There is no time frame to impermanence. Some changes can be sensed within seconds, while others may never be noticed in our brief lifetime. Contemplate the impermanence you may find in images that you already have in your album, or make new images over a short period of time and notice the variations. Let your creative lens lead the way.

When words fail us or are difficult to find in fully expressing our emotions, images may be less demanding, while they also can awaken latent creativity, inviting us to further explore and accept our emotions. This does not only imply difficult and grievous emotions. Changes and transitions may also bring up emotions of new possibilities, new relationships, and a widening road of our creative potential. Even if we at first may feel that we are not able to speak our truth, with time we may look to expand on our experience. That is when creative art activities may provide an additional vocabulary to help us find our voice when expressing our excitement or articulating our losses.

When losing a person we love, we can honor our beloved by creating an image that embodies the essence of that person's life. The created image could be a drawing or a collage of images that will continue to have a certain visual meaning to us. We have a need to talk about our loss but may find it difficult to express our feelings to a friend in a way that fully encompasses our emotions. Sharing a collage or painting with others may help both them and us to develop a deeper understanding of our loss.

Helen was in her early fifties when she suddenly lost her younger brother Nick to a stroke. Nick experienced his stroke while on a wilderness trek in Nepal, a destination that had been on Nick's bucket list for a long time. Nick was well acquainted with the first symptoms of a stroke from his work as a medic back home. Experiencing the heat going down his left arm, Nick immediately realized that he was experiencing a small stroke and that he should get help as soon as possible. But by the time he finally arrived at the local hospital, he'd suffered a second stroke and could not be helped back to life. When I met Helen about a year after the loss of her brother, she told me that not a day goes by that she does not think about and "talk" to her brother, whom she had always been very close to. After making a collage of her unspoken words of losing Nick, she expressed to me:

> *As an older sister, I always felt responsible for Nick, and he would always come to me when he needed to have a discussion. We could talk about anything, and somehow, we would know what the other person was thinking or going through. Losing Nick, I feel as if I have lost part of my soul, and that is what hurts more than anything. After my own husband died over ten years ago, and Nick was alone after a recent divorce, we became even closer. We began traveling together. We enjoyed the same kind of music, poetry, and food. We had so much fun planning and researching our destinations. We enjoyed learning about new places, different cultures, and just life! Even though I know that Nick is not with me in a physical sense, I also now know that he will always be with me for as long as I live, and for this I am so grateful. It is a paradox. Difficult to explain. But in making this collage, it was as if we were creating this together, as if Nick helped me to choose the images. It is as if I feel lighter now when I don't have to carry all my emotions inside of me, but now I can visualize what we had and still have together with a wider perspective. I sense this opening into a larger and endless experience, and the image brings me something new every time that I walk by the collage that now hangs in my hallway. I meet Nick on the way out and coming home on the way in, he is there for me.*

Exercise: My Losses and How They Changed Me

Spend twenty minutes writing:

Name one loss that you remember from childhood.

- How did this loss change your perspective?

Name one loss that you experienced as an adolescent.

- How did this loss change your perspective?

Name one loss you have experienced as an adult.

- How did this loss change your perspective?

Loss Is an Individual Experience

How people make meaning of events and emotions is uniquely personal and depends on an individual's experiences and present perception of their contextual meanings and personal control. Psychologist and author of *Stress and Coping*, Richard Lazarus, believes that our personal access to coping is based on previous mental, emotional, and motivational faculties. After our appraisal of a situation, whether we consider it to be positive, dangerous, or irrelevant, we analyze what sufficient or insufficient resources are available to best handle the situation. The next step in how we meet a stressful situation becomes either problem-focused (change situation itself) or emotion-focused (change relation to the situation). Breaking down the process of our reaction to stress this way, into slow motion, is not something that we are able to notice in real time. Nor is it something that comes to mind in our everyday lives. But it may be helpful to get a glimmer into our own emotional process so that we can meet stress in a way that is meaningful and can benefit our well-being.

Dr. Elisabeth Kübler-Ross (1926–2004) was a psychiatrist who pioneered in near-death studies with her seminal book *On Death and Dying* (1969). In the 1950s, when working with cancer patients, Kübler-Ross encouraged them to talk about their emotional process of being diagnosed with cancer. Before this time, there was an overpowering stigma around the word *cancer* because the general population believed it was tantamount to death, and death at that time was too scary to talk about. It was a taboo where even the word *cancer* was not mentioned but instead called "the Big C."

Through her patients, Kübler-Ross became familiar with the different stages of change and grief that individuals tend to go through after their cancer diagnosis. These stages have become known as DABDA (Denial, Anger, Bargaining, Depression, Acceptance). Later in her work, Kübler-Ross came to believe that these stages do not have to come in a special order, and that not all people who grieve a loss necessarily go through all these stages.

In the 1970s, Dr. Jimmie Holland began her work as a psycho-oncologist at Memorial Sloan Kettering in New York, where she treated patients in distress from cancer diagnosis. In her book *The Human Side of Cancer: Living with Hope, Coping with Uncertainty*, Holland confirms both from a scientific standpoint as well as from patients' personal stories that there is no such thing as a "one-size fits-all approach to coping with adversity but that everyone has a unique way of coping, which should be respected." During the years that I worked as an art therapist at Memorial Sloan Kettering, I was fortunate in that Dr. Holland was one of my supervisors. We would meet once a week, and we often spoke about the importance of finding a vehicle that would allow for the safe expression of our emotions. In discussing a creative outlet, she had noticed some of her patients had experienced a sense of freedom when letting go of themselves to see where creativity could lead them. When struggling with new limitations such as a life-threatening illness and loss, drawing or painting can be liberating and lead to a boost in our self-esteem with a sense of personal control over our circumstances.

I was first introduced to the transformative power of art therapy by Dr. Paola Luzzatti, psychologist and art therapist. In the late 1990s, Dr. Luzzatti pioneered the introduction of art therapy to patients at Memorial Sloan Kettering. During my two-year internship under Dr. Luzzatti's guidance, I had the privilege of observing, practicing, and learning how creative engagement can bring deeply held, unspoken emotions to the surface. This process fosters a new understanding for the creator, which can lead to peace, openness, and emotional healing. It's important to distinguish healing from curing, as the latter follows its own unique process and outcomes. I am deeply grateful to Dr. Luzzatti for sharing her knowledge, inspiration, and unwavering support, which encouraged me to pursue my passion for promoting health and healing through the creative expression of emotions.

Working or engaging in a creative field can feel isolating, and solitude is often a natural part of the creative process. It is in those quiet, still moments that we may uncover what our soul truly needs to express. However, when feelings of emptiness or loneliness arise, I have found that nature restores my energy and rekindles my creative enthusiasm. I also make it a priority to attend local art shows or theater performances near my village, as they never fail to inspire and invigorate me. As a side note, I would like to take a moment to emphasize the importance of seeking out the energy and enthusiasm of those who share our aspirations and visionary spirit whenever possible.

During difficult times—whether facing illness, divorce, or loss—many people seek the support of others who are experiencing something similar. Patients in the hospital's support groups have often shared with me how much they looked forward to these gatherings. In the group, they could express their emotions freely, speaking their minds without fear of judgment or the need to censor themselves. There was no comparison of feelings, no pressure to measure their pain against others. Instead, they found strength in listening to each other's stories, recognizing both the shared human experience and the deeply personal nature of their own journey.

There is also the situation where groups and sharing with other individuals can make us feel even more vulnerable. Maybe the level of pain in the group is more than some feel comfortable with or find helpful. This is when it is very important to listen to what genuinely works for us as individuals and not judge or compare ourselves to others.

Expressions of self-knowledge call us to action. 'Know Thyself' was written over the portal of the antique world, more than two thousand years after the seven sages inscribed it on the forecourt of their oracle. Over the portal of the new world, 'Be Thyself' shall be written.

—Oscar Wilde

Creativity Moves Us Through Loss

In his poem *Winter Grief,* poet David Whyte reflects on how grief draws us into movement—not to escape, but to remember. When faced with pain we cannot mend, we walk to honor what was, even the memories we might rather forget. Most of us find it difficult, and sometimes with a feeling that we're never going to get over it, to move through a time of personal loss. But when we slowly let an event take its course without any judgment or wishes of a particular result, we may find a new opening. This may begin with just a glimpse of something shifting inside of us, a new feeling of hope, or a different possibility than the one we had previously been telling ourselves.

Ron, a fifty-five-year-old construction foreman, lost movement in both his legs after a spinal cord injury. A temporary landing on a four-story building that Ron and a colleague were inspecting moved suddenly, sending both men to the ground. Ron's friend and colleague had died from the fall, while Ron was still alive but unconscious when the medics reached them. Ron not only suffered multiple injuries but also lost his friend and colleague, his physical abilities, and his job, as well as his dream for a future that included hiking the mountains of different countries.

During my first meeting with Ron, he was sitting in a wheelchair and looking out over a wide garden. He looked strong and energetic as he told me his story:

> *When I woke up and regained consciousness at the hospital after the horrible fall from the building, I was devastated. For weeks, I was just lying in bed, looking down at my legs that would not move. Well, after five weeks, I was discharged from the hospital in a wheelchair. Luckily for me, my wonderful wife had organized our home to accommodate my incapacity to move. That is when I first realized how fortunate I was, but not being able to fully take in that emotion, I could not find the words. My life had changed in ways that I could not have imagined, and now there was another life, a new life, a new road that was unfamiliar, slightly frightening, with a feeling of loneliness. Loneliness in my situation. Three years have passed, and I will always think about my partner, but I will also remember the good times we had together, and he is still with me in so many ways. What came to me, one day about a year ago, despite my losses, was a wake-up call to the fact that*

I had not lost my joy for life, and I began to think that I owed it both to my friend and to myself to embark on our dreams of hiking the mountains. Yes, I know, that seemed quite impossible without the help of two legs, but then I was thinking of other ways. Long story short, I found a group of other handicapped people who were looking for new adventures with their "new normal" bodies. We are meeting at least once a week, most of the time over Zoom. This group has made all the difference to my new life, and now we are organizing a trip to the Andes Mountains.

It can be challenging to grasp and connect to what it is that we are truly feeling after a loss, besides a sense of confusion, disappointment, grief, and general bewilderment. We may find it difficult to talk about these issues with friends, family, or professionals such as a therapist or chaplain. This is the time when we can find solace and respite from our tired mind by allowing ourselves to apply our creative side as an interlude and helping hand in expressing our emotions.

Some find peace in listening to or composing music. Others may join a support group, as Ron did. We may feel a whole different environment is meeting us as we move through a loss. We remind ourselves that this is the new ground that we are standing on. This is the solid ground that, for the present, is our trusted ally. Some may notice that an intense new interest in life emerges, an interest that may now be moving in a different direction than the previous one. Others may cope with the loss by enhancing a previous activity that has been dormant for a long time. We may not need to start from scratch to find that firm ground beneath our feet. Maybe what reemerges is something that already feels grounding and familiar, but we approach it with a renewed purpose. As the spiritual teacher and author Eckhart Tolle writes in his book *A New Earth*, "Some changes look negative on the surface, but you will soon realize that space is being created in your life for something new to emerge."

Marianne experienced this reemergence. She became deeply depressed after the death of her husband of more than fifty years. In her younger years, Marianne loved to draw and worked as a fashion designer. But after marriage and with a busy family life of four children, she had not been able to use her creative skills for many years. When I met Marianne at a recent event, she told me: "A few years ago, I had a deep depression. The only therapy I believe in is to paint. I began to paint myself out of depression. After seven days and seven nights, I felt good again. And I had made 230 sketches . . . even though I had not painted for over thirty years." She later showed me some of her drawings and beautiful, loosely painted sketches of models in colorful, sweeping gowns.

Even if we have not had a creative profession as our livelihood, we all know how to use a crayon or watercolor. Choose a color or use any other creative outlet that expresses your wordless emotions to start toward a new reality and a new joyful and creative focus in life.

Finding Stillness in Making Art

While we are active in a purposeful creative activity, we also create a gap in our thinking. When we stay focused on our process, we simply move from one color, one tone, one movement to the next and the next . . . and without thinking, we later realize that we have given ourselves moments of stillness from our mind. This may be a new feeling and, much like the practice of meditation, something that we can repeat and build on.

After an emotional or traumatic experience, emotions that are held in our body may not be consciously recognized and accepted until some time has passed. During one session in a recent workshop, Carina was working on her two paintings for the "chaos to calm" exercise, where she stayed silently focused on the process of moving through the guiding prompts. After she had finished and we observed her images from a short distance, she reflected on her experience:

> *In the first image of chaos, all those dots are my intruding thoughts that I simply cannot seem to get away from, or to keep quiet. They are there all the time, all those little brown dots. But then, in making the second image of calm, it was as if I found an opening, where there are no dots, no thoughts; it was such a relief. It was as if my mind felt cleansed for a while, and in that red space is where I have found calm, at least for now . . .*
>
> *I came to this group with expectations, and I was not disappointed. I am in a personal crisis right now as a widow. My husband died last year after we were together for seventy years . . . it is unbearable that he is no longer alive . . . so I am very vulnerable in different ways, but I thought the circle was positive and interesting. I have never experienced anything like this . . . a whole new experience and way of thinking for me. I enjoyed getting to know the people in the group, on a different level than when we just meet at dinner or in playing cards. When my husband lived, we had an active social life, and we were always together . . . always . . . maybe that was not the best thing in the end. Now, when I think about it, maybe that is why it is hard to learn to be alone . . . he was always there; we even worked together. I never dreamt that I would feel so lonely, even here in the senior residence with so many people around. I am learning to accept my new life, but it is hard work, to have to go down for dinner, to be outgoing, and try to be a friend.*

Before I used to say: I take it one day at a time . . . now I say, I take it an hour at a time . . . that helps my mind . . . otherwise, I get a sense of panic, as if going down into an abyss. This is the first time that I have used red since my husband died. The chaos and difficulties that I have felt around me the last year cannot reach me anymore. I painted myself into the comfort of a cocoon, where I am resting in the calmness of one color. It feels like a great liberation, and that is what I will name my painting.

Here is a brief description of Carina's paintings and a few symbolic references to what red may signify for her:

- Carina's initial painting of "chaos" features a bright yellow background with scattered dark brown dots, creating a textured, almost organic feel. At the center, there is an irregularly shaped form outlined in black, resembling an island or footprint, with a bold red interior. Within this red shape, a smaller square shape is drawn with a black outline. This smaller shape is what Carina later used for her second painting. The overall effect of her initial painting is both abstract and symbolic, evoking themes of isolation, grounding, or a focal point amidst a larger landscape. The warm, energetic color palette gives the piece a vibrant and expressive quality.
- Carina's second painting, equal in size to her first, is a vast red color field—a magnified version of the small square she had outlined in her initial piece. With large, sweeping brushstrokes, the red fills the entire canvas, leaving no empty space or unpainted borders. After completing both paintings and taking a moment of silent reflection, Carina realized that

together, they embodied a powerful and deeply personal transformation—one that resonated with her journey of healing.

As discussed previously, when contemplating held messages in symbols, color, words, or other creative expressions, they are all personal perspectives based on our lifelong experiences and memories, whether conscious or unconscious. That said, the following few guidelines may lead to further insight into your own artwork. For someone experiencing recent loss, red can hold a range of deep and complex emotions, for example:

- Intense grief and emotional pain: Red is often associated with strong, raw emotions. In the context of loss, it can symbolize the deep, sometimes overwhelming pain of mourning, especially in the early stages when feelings are most intense.
- Love and connection: Red is also the color of the heart, symbolizing the deep love and bond shared with the person who is no longer physically present. It may represent how that connection endures, even through grief.
- Anger and restlessness: Loss can bring up frustration, unresolved feelings, or even anger—toward circumstances, oneself, or the situation. Red can express this emotional turbulence and the difficulty of processing change.
- Vitality and life force: Despite its association with pain, red is also a color of strength and resilience. It may reflect the energy still present in the mourner, a reminder of their own life force and ability to continue forward, even in sorrow.

- A call for expression: Red demands attention; it does not retreat. In grief, it can symbolize the need to acknowledge and express emotions rather than suppress them. The presence of red in a personal work of art might be an unconscious way of bringing those feelings to the surface.

That Carina titled her second painting *Liberation* is such a powerful transformation. Her journey from avoidance to full immersion in red speaks volumes about the healing process through creative expression. Initially, red may have represented pain, grief, or even an unbearable intensity of emotion—something too overwhelming to face. As Carina mentioned above, after her husband's death, she could not bear to have the color red in her home or to wear any red clothes. By gradually reintroducing it into her work and eventually embracing it as a dominant color, she seems to have moved toward integration rather than avoidance.

A large red color field suggests a deep surrender to emotion, a willingness to fully inhabit the color rather than resist it. Instead of being something painful to avoid, red has now become a space she can step into, perhaps even a source of strength, joy, or renewal.

Exercise: Finding Stillness in Images

Warm-up Writing:

Spend ten minutes writing your imaginary experience of:

- When I got stranded on a deserted island, I . . .
- The first time a bird landed on my shoulder, it was . . .

Materials:

Two boards or pieces of paper (approximately 16 x 24 inches)
Glue stick
Ten to fifteen images cut out of magazines

Instructions:

In Carina's image, she used paint to express her loss, challenge, and renewal, but here we will expand on this exercise by including images.

Spend forty-five minutes on making two collages:

- *Collage #1:* Images or words that represent a sense of loss and the challenges of transitions.
- *Collage #2:* Images or words that evoke renewal and hope.

When looking for images in magazines, cut out those images that speak to you without thinking about why. When your eyes are drawn to an image, choose it even if your thinking mind is not in favor. Remember, you are open to an experience where your mind does not censor your actions and your eyes have a life of their own. This is where your core/soul is making the decisions.

1. Spend ten minutes collecting images for Collage #1. Then spend ten minutes collecting images for Collage #2.
2. Make a second collection by bringing the number of your chosen images for each collage down to ten to fifteen pieces.
3. Arrange the images on your board/paper. You may leave space between some images, while others may want to overlap.
4. Use the glue stick to attach each image to your board.
5. Give your collages titles. Then attach them to a wall in front of you for silent observation.

Exercise Reflection:

When we title our work on the exercises in this book, we don't do it for anybody but ourselves. The titles are not words for submitting to an art gallery or for a search engine find. No, they are the uncensored words of your own emotional, spiritual, and intellectual experience that may transform into an ongoing conversation with Self. A title may be in the form of one word or a sentence based on freedom of imagination. When we free ourselves from social pressure and the judging mind, that's the time to quickly write down the words that come to us. Even though they may not mean much in the moment, after some time, those words will elucidate their story and bring further insight and depth to our artwork.

After observing your collages for about five minutes, write a paragraph or two about what the images/words say to you. Leave the collages in a place where you may see them from time to time. After one week, come back to your journal and write a second sentiment about your artwork. Notice if there is a continued story from your initial journaling.

Coping with Pet Loss

A dog can never tell you what she knows from the
smells of the world, but you know, watching her,
that you know
almost nothing.

—Mary Oliver

Those of us who love and adore our pets will most likely experience their death. Pets give us comfort and companionship that is ever-present and nonjudgmental. That is why their loss is so difficult. We have become used to their physical form, their movements, and their personalities. Although we always knew in some abstract form that they would die, our mind doesn't always accept their death as reality. And the loss of our pet may further be a reminder of previous losses in our life and thereby amplify our sadness. We grieve the loss of their death, but as Eckhart Tolle would remind us: While we experience pain from the emptiness that they leave behind, if we can become aware of their formlessness that remains with us, our continuous bond will help us cope with the inevitable impermanence of all living beings.

When my own beloved dog Skye died, I was devastated and inconsolable. I was not able to listen to well-meaning friends and family members making suggestions that I was not ready to hear. There is indeed no timeline for ending grief, no "right" time to get back to normal. There is a new normal that will never fully be as life was before our loss. For some, a continuous bond in a formless sense of relationship may be what is part of our new normal. Others may find that they need to close a door behind them, at least for a time. Moving through a significant loss will always entail complexities and sometimes unexpected emotions, which, when accepted, will support us on our journey of living and learning.

Below is a shortened eulogy that came through me a few weeks after Skye had died. When deciding to write his short story, it truly felt as if Skye did the writing, smoothly and continuously. After the writing, I experienced a shift from the almost crippling sense of loss to an acceptance of reality and a gratitude that I had enjoyed many years with my beloved puppy. I am sharing this here in hopes of helping others who also have had or will have to go through the challenges of loss, sadness, and sometimes a sense of guilt from helping their ill and/or older pet to leave this life.

SKYE

6/12/1998 to 8/17/2009

After some thinking, I decided to write my own brief eulogy from my very joyous sojourn to planet Earth. Mom took a picture of me about one month before I left Earth. If you could see this photo, you would know that I had a real good time out in the archipelago, wearing my new fitted life vest and sitting on the bridge of my uncle's passenger boat, overlooking the vast sea life.

My journey here on Earth began in Florida, where Mom met me at a breeder who took care of my family and me. Well, right then and there, I decided to leave with Mom, who took me to her house. I was only about eight weeks old when I met Mom and did not have a real name, so Mom decided to give me a naming ceremony (well, I let her) in the birdbath (!) in the garden. I was named "Out-of-Skye," which became Skye for short, and her wish during the ceremony was that "my presence would bring joy to all whom I came in contact with."

Little did she know the joy that I received from all whom I met in my travels. If they let me, I would give thousands of kisses. If not, I still had a chance of connecting to them via their shoes. My favorite routine was to grab a newly stepped out of shoe, run as fast as I could, pull the insole out and throw it up in the air, and hopefully make the non-kissable shoe-owners happy in a different way. Sometimes it worked. At least they would remember me when they walked out of the house in a different level shoe than what they came in with.

Of course, I had my jobs and responsibilities to take care of. I protected the abode and Mom wherever she took me. I would "know" and hear anybody who came within sniffing distance and immediately alert Mom that something potentially was about to take place. I also made sure that Mom got up before six every morning and strongly suggested to her that it would be most appropriate to go to sleep with the sun around nine every night. Another responsibility that I took very seriously was my daily beauty sleep, which took a couple of hours every morning after breakfast, especially during the later years. A routine that I highly recommend to all my friends. My friends, I am lucky to say, are numerous. Friends, families, and caregivers have a big place in my heart and will always be with me wherever I go from here.

Mom asked the veterinarian that my body be cremated and that one of my favorite toys, a little white bear, be cremated with me so I know that I will never be alone. I was diagnosed with a form of blood disorder that depleted both my platelets and red blood cells, and my body was not able to respond to any remedies or treatments. This is the first time in my life that I was ill and did not know that I was "diagnosed," so I was happy, although a little tired from all the meds, and gave Mom plenty of kisses minutes before my heart stopped.

Well, I am off to see some of my friends that I have not seen for a while. You may remember some of them as Mrs. B, Fred, Amber, Bear, and Eliesha.

Thank you all. Much joy, much laughter, and much cuddly and heartfelt love to all my two-footed and four-footed friends who still walk the earth!

Yours forever, Skye

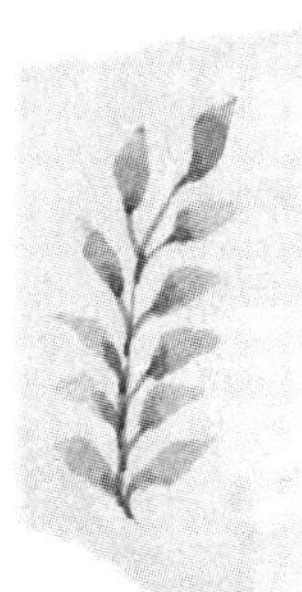

Chapter Eleven

Nurturing the Joyful Life

Waking up to new discoveries about ourselves and our deeper passions is what brings joy at midlife. Some of us may find that we resist changes, such as when our children leave home, when we no longer spend our time on our careers, or when the comfort of our workplace with the familiar faces of our colleagues is no longer part of our everyday environment. Our challenge is to look joyously into the new possibilities instead of worrying about what we are leaving behind. By connecting to our creative self, we can find an inner guide to carry us onward, forward, and inward to new hope and possibilities. The curiosity and intensity that we devote to a new passion make all the difference to how deeply we will be able to connect to that part of ourselves, where we truly feel, sense, and *know* that our truth is real. Author Hugh Walpole wrote in *Reading an Essay*: "The whole secret of life is to be interested in one thing profoundly and a thousand other things well."

Some of us may recognize ourselves in Walpole's statement. I have certainly found the pull in myself to embark on new interests, new roads, and new experiences. In reaching midlife, when most people begin to downsize and spend fewer hours working, it seemed I went the opposite direction. From the comfort of a well-appointed apartment in a city with all the amenities, there was still something that did not speak to my expressive soul. I missed the closeness of nature and being able to walk outside upon awakening, listening to the birds, and enjoying the lack of man-made noises. So, I followed my impulse by moving to a larger home with an old overgrown garden in a small village. I had to relearn what it takes to be the caretaker of both house and land. Some things had to be left behind, such as friends, familiar routines, and well-known geography, and that is sad. But this also must be part of our moving ahead. What may seem like a loss at the time can change shape and become a new relationship and connection. No matter our age, we can always connect to that curiosity and vitality within that lead us forward to new learning, experiences, and creative activities when we look at the environment through our artful and expressive lens.

If we are curious about life, there will always be something or someone pulling at us, promising new adventures and riches in learning. Diversity in experiences is what brings fullness and joy to our lifestyle. In midlife, this may be the first time that we truly feel the confidence and freedom to pursue new interests. Something that we may previously have just touched upon in our younger life when our goals, dreams, and aspirations were different. But when we become clear on what truly matters to us while editing out those activities that don't, we will find that we have better access to our purpose and begin to flourish. This will not only enhance our own well-being and joy but will also become like rings on the water, moving in ever-widening circles, benefiting others around us. We can leave a legacy to younger generations as models of what to look forward to in a world that currently may not inspire a great deal of positive creative freedom. As poet Emily Dickinson wrote, "I dwell in possibilities." Her words might serve as a wonderful reminder upon waking up every morning of how to live out the rest of our lives. Creativity, as we now know, is rich with unexpected possibilities.

Where Next?

This surrealistic image of *Where Next?* was created by Theo during a weeklong photography workshop, where one of the activities involved experimenting with double exposures. Having recently retired from his career as a biology teacher, Theo was eager to embrace new adventures, particularly in hiking areas he had never explored before. Photography had long been a cherished hobby, and now, with more time on his hands, he wanted to deepen his connection to it—not just as a way to document nature, but as a means of artistic expression. His goal was to move beyond pure documentation and use his camera to tell stories that resonated more deeply with his creative voice.

When looking at Theo's image, you will see a striking double exposure or digital blending of a majestic bird of prey, possibly a falcon or eagle, and the lush canopy of a tree. The bird's form is seamlessly merged with the tree, creating a layered effect where its body and wings appear to be composed of branches and foliage. The bird's head remains distinct, with its sharp beak and focused eye giving a sense of strength, clarity, and vision. The background consists of a soft gradient sky, transitioning from pale blue to gentle green, with hints of clouds adding depth and atmosphere. This ethereal setting enhances the dreamlike quality of the image, as if the bird and tree exist in a liminal space between reality and imagination.

It is clear in this image that Theo has moved beyond a documentary representation to a level of imagination where form, object, and color take on a new life and energy of their own. While being in the midst of creating his image, it is, however, not clear if Theo was conscious of the symbolic interpretations that his image might have held for him. If we look at the image from Carl Jung's theories on the collective unconscious and archetypes, he might have seen an interesting image that goes far beyond a bird or a tree. Jung believed that certain symbols, such as birds, trees, water, and colors, are universally embedded in human consciousness and appear in myths, dreams, and art across cultures.

If we examine Theo's image through a combination of psychological, artistic, cultural, and literary lenses, several possible interpretations emerge. However, since I do not know Theo well enough to claim insight into his personal intentions, I approach the image with an open-ended perspective. When someone feels uncertain about how to engage with their own painting, photograph, or dream, I often guide them by saying, **"If this were my image, I might wonder . . ."**—offering a starting point without imposing meaning.

This method invites deeper self-exploration, encouraging individuals to see beyond the purely objective aspects of composition, balance, and color theory. It becomes an exercise in expanding perception, stepping outside conditioned ways of seeing, and allowing intuition to lead. When we take that **courageous leap beyond learned conventions**, we enter a realm of **infinite possibility**—a space where creativity flows freely. In doing so, we may find that doors, once locked by rigid expectations, swing open from their long-rusted hinges, revealing a renewed sense of wonder and artistic joy.

Here are a few symbolically leading starting points that might be noticed when observing Theo's image: The bird represents freedom, perspective, intuition, and transformation. Birds of prey are often associated with keen vision and the ability to see the bigger picture. They are known for their sharp eyesight, able to spot the smallest movement from incredible distances. This ability has long been a metaphor for clarity, foresight, and wisdom. Birds are further known to symbolize the power that helps people speak reflectively and leads them to think out many things in advance before they take action. Unconsciously, humans are drawn to this idea—the dream of seeing beyond the present moment, of gaining perspective over life's complexities. The bird's constant movement, soaring through vast landscapes, shifting effortlessly between earth and sky, may be seen as mirroring the human experience of change, transformation, and the search for meaning. In dreams and art, birds often represent the ability to move beyond constraints, whether physical, emotional, or psychological.

In the image, the bird's gaze is sharp and focused, yet its body is merged with organic earthly elements. The tree, as discussed previously, symbolizes grounding, growth, and resilience. It suggests a deep rooted connection to nature, strength, and endurance through life's changes. The bird's gaze into the distance could reflect an unconscious recognition that while we strive for big-picture vision and clarity, we remain tethered to the environment, our past, and our lived experiences. There is often an inherent duality in the human spirit—a need for stability and a yearning for exploration. Birds, with their fluid movement and endless perspective, embody both these aspects. This image, whether intentional or not, reflects an unconscious awareness of this duality. There is the desire to move freely and embrace change (represented by the bird's wings and expansive vision). And there is also the need to stay connected to something solid and familiar (represented by the tree's structure and deep roots).

The fusion of these two elements (the bird of prey and the tree) suggests that true vision is not only about seeing far but about understanding where we stand. The boundless sky and the rooted earth are not opposing forces but part of the same journey—one that requires balance between movement and stillness, freedom and connection, vision, and presence. Drawing from my own work in the creative process and expressive art therapy, creative personal works are often a reflection of inner experience rather than just aesthetic choices. In Theo's case of being newly retired, his transition from structure (biology teaching) to creative exploration (photography) suggests that his subconscious is working through change, blending his old identity with his new path, leading to further learning, deeper insight, and a joyful way of being.

Exercise: Where Do I Fly To?

Using markers, pencils, or a brush, create an imaginary landscape of flying on to your next journey.

Expand your imagination and let go of your rational thinking mind while observing your flying self. Do you see yourself as a winged horse? An eagle? Or are you standing tall or lounging on a flying magic carpet? Or . . .?

Reflect on bringing the imagined sense of freedom to the ground on which you stand. How do you see this freedom manifested in your everyday life? What is your creative expression? Write for fifteen minutes.

Creative Expressions Lead to Self-Renewal

Expressing ourselves creatively and through our artful lens can take many different forms, from visual arts, music and sound, dance movements, writing, and sewing to making meals, creative cooking, or baking. Creative activities often have an element of repair to them, helping to reduce feelings of sadness or remorse and replacing those feelings with something that is restorative and joyful.

Sylvia had recently turned fifty-six when her older husband, George, suffered a stroke, which left him using a wheelchair. They had no other choice but to sell their farmhouse and move into a small apartment that could accommodate George's disability. He was unable to take care of himself. Sylvia left her job to become the full-time caretaker until George had to be moved to assisted living five years later. Sylvia had at times felt resentful, never being able to pursue her creative joy of painting, baking, and sewing while she was taking care of George. But now, without that caretaking purpose, Sylvia felt depressed, tired, and uncertain about what to do with her life when she was no longer needed 24/7. She had been fulfilled with a purpose when caring for her husband. Losing her identity as a wife and caretaker, she now realized that it had meant a great deal to her. Sylvia slowly began to realize why she now had such low energy and felt listless. With George no longer under her full-time care, there was a sudden vacuum of purpose and meaning in her life. The routines that supported her every day were no longer there.

Sylvia knew that she had to go on with her life, but struggled to think of anything worthwhile and spent most of her days in the apartment, reading or watching television. As a homemaker, Sylvia loved to be creative in the kitchen and bake for her family and friends. After some time, she slowly began to create beautiful baked goods that she brought to the nursing home where George now lived. By reconnecting to her love of baking, Sylvia felt her old vitality and energy coming back. The word spread of

Sylvia's tasty and appealing cakes, and she began receiving orders for sale. Today, Sylvia has many happy customers, and she has a newfound purpose and ongoing joy serving them.

Living Creatively Leads to More Joyful Days

In an article titled "The Science Behind Creativity," Kirsten Weir summarizes research performed by various scientists whose studies are connected to health and the arts at different ages. In conclusion, Weir notes four prompts that are included in the discussed research on how to become more creative:

1. *Put in the work:* People often think of creativity as a bolt of inspiration, like a lightbulb clicking on. But being creative in a particular domain—whether in the arts, in your work, or in your day-to-day life—is a skill. Carve out time to learn and practice.
2. *Let your mind wander:* Experts recommend "daydreaming with purpose." Make opportunities to let your daydreams flow, while gently nudging them toward the creative challenge at hand. Some research suggests meditation may help people develop the habit of purposeful daydreaming.
3. *Practice remote associations:* Brainstorm ideas, jotting down whatever thoughts or notions come to you, no matter how wild. You can always edit later.
4. *Go outside:* Spending time in nature and wide-open spaces can expand your attention, enhance beneficial mind-wandering, and boost creativity.
5. *Revisit your creative ideas:* Aha moments can give you a high—but that rush might make you overestimate the merit of a creative idea. Don't be afraid to revisit ideas to critique and tweak them later.

These prompts sum up what we have already discussed in the previous chapters. We are all "researchers" as we enjoy our creative activities and take notice of what we are feeling, what our progress is, and what is next! We may notice how the act of expressing ourselves creatively often fosters a sense of purpose and accomplishment. There is no more powerful way to connect to ourselves than by our own creative expression and interpretation of what we have made. Using your artful lens can help you uncover and nurture your inner joys and dreams and make them real.

As we have discussed in earlier chapters, we are highly diverse and pulled in different directions to what seemingly will bring us joy, new insight, and new possibilities. In meeting our own complex nature through artful activities, we may come across heretofore hidden treasures and become startled by our own creative callings.

In my own life, I have been fortunate to meet with a great deal of diverse experiences and changes, most of them unexpected. Some have not seemed either fortunate or joyful at the time. But like a large interwoven tapestry, our individual combined experiences manifest as the most exquisite and intriguing work of art, where none is like another and where your tapestry shines the brightest of them all. This may sound excessive at first, as we have become used to judging and minimizing our own progress, failures, and successes rather than seeing them as a contribution to our overall experience and learning. But as we have witnessed through the art exercises we have completed so far, there will always be new creative paths to discover.

Exercise: Finding Joy in the Creative Flow

In this final exercise using your smartphone, the aim is to find a flow in your images. Do they hold together as a story? Do they have something to tell? If so, what? Find a place, an object, or an environment that calls for your attention. Then immerse yourself fully in this stunning location/object and explore every nook and cranny. Focus on the minute details as well as the bigger picture. Build on the smartphone exercises from previous chapters or follow your own creative impulse. Select four images from this exercise, title your work, and write a short fictional story of your *place.* Maybe your place is a building, a flowerpot on your windowsill, a place in the garden, or a river that elicits stories.

Creativity Is Our Empowered Path to Positive Experiences

Creativity is the most powerful way to connect to ourselves, our inner strength, vitality, and self-worth. How can we not embrace this relatively simple yet so necessary road to empowerment?

Research on the connection between creativity and health is a relatively new field. My own research as a health psychologist on the biological, psychological, and social impact of engaging in creative artwork has proved to be an eye-opener, both to myself and to those patients and workshop participants with whom I have been fortunate to share many hours of newfound creative possibilities. Previously, physiological information was only available to a certain segment of the population studying medicine. However, today many of us have become used to finding information on physiological, biological, or social questions through our own research, albeit on a surface level, through the internet. We have questions. We want to know what and why engaging in creativity is important to our overall health. What can creativity do for us? Is there a science behind creativity?

Dr. Gene Cohen found through his studies that creativity contributes to physical health as we age. He found that the interaction of our released emotions, our brain function, and our immune system during creative pursuits suggests a positive outlook and a sense of well-being that in turn contribute to our overall health.

Similarly, Dr. Jeremy Nobel, the founder and president of the Foundation for Art and Healing, believes that engaging in creative arts modulates brain activities and induces a cascade of neurotransmitters associated with pleasure and reward. Other scientific studies have shown that engaging in creative arts can lead to an increase in the feel-good neurotransmitters, such as serotonin, dopamine, endorphins, and oxytocin, that contribute to mood regulation and social bonding. Listening to music or simply observing art that you enjoy has a direct impact on your level of cortisol, the stress hormone, effectively reducing stress.

Mitch was brought up by an authoritarian father who insisted on him becoming a great soccer player. He was always told by his parents how strong, fast, and athletic he was. And that he should expect scholarships to college because he would be good for the team. Mitch was the middle sibling between two sisters, both of whom were more inclined to poetry, dancing, and painting. Mitch's mother was a well-known painter. According to his father's wish, Mitch went through his academic years all paid for by athletic scholarships. Graduating at the top of his class, he had no problem landing a well-paid position in a high-powered investment firm. During his years as an executive, although he enjoyed his work, his colleagues, and his responsibilities, there was always an underlying feeling of something missing. He would keenly feel this when visiting his sisters, who were now accomplished creative artists. Mitch was worried when noticing a new transition during the last couple of years. He was feeling a loss in vitality, was more tired than normal, and did not wake up looking forward to a day at the office. A physical check with his general practitioner had proven all good values, and Mitch was given a green light of good physical health.

When I met Mitch, he was in his late fifties, and he had enrolled in a four-week course on creativity in the workplace, where the aim was to empower creative ideas to flow without judgment and barriers. The focus was on creative ideas that would still be considered productive and meaningful to himself, his colleagues, and his employer. One exercise was designed to help build on a new relationship with himself.

At the end of one day of class, Mitch was silently reflecting on his newly created images. After taking some time to observe the images that were now attached to a wall in front of him, there was one image that Mitch felt most clearly spoke to him:

> *When I was in the process of cutting out pieces, it was immediately the physical perception of myself as the strong male that came to me. And then, of course, it was soccer that had been a big part of my life and in many ways formed me during those important years of adolescence and young adulthood. I learned a great deal also about camaraderie, respect, and working together as a team, which has been helpful to me as a manager in the workplace, where I have many people depending on me.*
>
> *After cutting out images without thinking, it was as if the strong male image moved out from the dark into the light, realizing new opportunities and possibilities in the circles all around me. Circles that can mean so many more things than a football. But I can also see that I am not leaving my executive life behind. I am still keeping one foot in the life*

that has supported me all these years, while I am moving on to new possibilities in the relationship with myself. I will put this collage in my office as a reminder, even if I put it in a drawer for now and see it as a promise of joy to come, and that there is always an opening. I am thinking that I may even sign up for a course in graphic design . . . could actually be helpful even in my present position.

Here is a description of Mitch's artwork: This is an image on white paper in a bold and dynamic composition made from cut-out paper shapes, featuring three human-like figures in motion. The figures, primarily in blue, seem to be dancing, reaching, or moving forward against a background of scattered geometric and round shapes in red, green, and blue. The leftmost figure appears as a white silhouette, set against a deep blue background, as if emerging from or stepping out of one phase into another. The middle and right figures are fully formed in blues, suggesting movement, growth, or progression.

The scattered red, green, and blue shapes floating around the figures may symbolize external influences, challenges, or opportunities—elements in flux as the creator navigates life transitions. The energetic and fluid composition conveys a sense of transformation, of stepping into the unknown while interacting with one's surroundings in a playful or exploratory way.

Given that this artwork was made by Mitch—who, at the time, experienced loss of vitality and a longing to express the creative voice that lingered in his soul—it could reflect his journey through a transition. Perhaps, even unconsciously, Mitch created images of self in moving from an old identity to something new, gaining momentum, and embracing the possibilities ahead. The progression from the white silhouette to the fully formed blue figures could symbolize his reawakening creative self, moving from a space of emptiness or detachment into more engagement and vitality. The fact that Mitch chose bold colors and dynamic movement suggests that, deep down, there is still a strong creative force within him—one that may have been dormant but is not lost. His artwork seems to reflect an intuitive step toward reconnecting with that side of himself, even if he is not entirely sure how to begin. Sometimes, just making the first creative mark can open doors to further exploration and rediscovery.

Our Joyful Legacy

My aunt Ruthel recently died at the age of 101 years, 7 months, and 8 days. Ruthel lived a creative life as a painter of fashion for advertisements, long before the internet or digital photography. Her creative energy spilled over into how she maintained her home, her cooking, and her overall representation of what life had to offer, and likewise what it takes away. Well into her nineties, she would tell me that she was not ready to die; she wanted to know what was happening around her, wanted to learn more, to experience. She was curious. During her last decade of living, her physical body was declining and giving her a great deal of pain. Even so, I can still hear her laughter during our phone conversations. Thinking about Ruthel and the legacy she left behind brings me joy during our now "silent" conversations. Perhaps we don't realize how much we leave behind after our passing, in the way we meet challenges, how we show courage, and how we embrace creativity, which has the potential to give joy and hope to those who still walk the earth. Ruthel was only seventeen years old when she came to Sweden as a refugee from Berlin at the beginning of World War II. But as long as I have known her, she always looked forward; even though deeply wounded from what she left behind, she refused to let the past pain influence her current joy.

During the later years, Ruthel spent most of her awake time on top of her bed due to physical limitations. This is where she met her guests, looked through the daily mail, read the newspaper, took in her meals, and watched films on TV during the night when she would wake up. The small square night table next to her bed was covered with a clear glass top, and underneath the glass Ruthel had made a collage of images from different times of her life that brought back joy and heart-warming memories. The images that sparked memories of times and events often became the thread to our ongoing conversations. This practice of making a collage of photos from different times of our lives and being able to see them and embrace our different ages, rather than putting them away in a box, album, or digital hard-to-find place, made me curious to find out what would happen in making my own "shrine." What first felt slightly awkward turned out to be a fun-filled activity with renewed surprises and amazement at the vast richness and variations that fill all our lives. As Gertrude Stein (1874–1946), artist and author, wrote: "We are always the same age inside."

Exercise: Finding Continued Joy and Play in Mixed Media Expression

Warm-up Writing:

Spend ten minutes finishing a paragraph that begins:

- I have learned a great deal about my world through all the artful lens exercises, and I look at things differently now because . . .
- In my continued creative path, I can see myself being open to newfound joy and play such as . . .

Materials:

This exercise in mixed media involves using more than one art medium. Your choice may include such things as watercolors, felt tip pens, squiggles, rubber stamps, photos, illustrations from magazines, music scores, words, fabric, strings of yarn, dried leaves or branches picked up from a nature walk, or anything else that you have at home and would like to use for your collage. Allow your imagination to flow and enjoy the process without any attachment or projections of the result.

Instructions:

1. Sort out no more than ten pieces of material that you have collected and that you find your eyes moving toward.
2. Play with the pieces while allowing a free-flowing energy to move around on the top of a board, watercolor paper, or canvas. Allow yourself the freedom to be surprised as creative joy begins to take shape in the relationship between the forms of your artwork.

After you move your collage into an interesting composition, be ready to glue the pieces into their positions.

3. Use a glue stick or matte medium (e.g., Liquitex or Mod Podge) to glue everything down on your background. Only a small amount of matte medium is needed on a large brush while going over your image. If you want to create a certain mood, you can add acrylic paint to the matte medium, but try it out first on a separate clean paper to make sure this is the tone you desire.
4. After you finish your first mixed media expression, you may use this as a stepping stone in moving on to the next and the next as you keep learning and finding more joy in your creative path.

Exercise Reflection:

After you have allowed time to reflect and see deeper into your collage, write a short story of what you see in the movements, colors, and shapes. The more you write, observe, and listen, the more you will find in your creative expression. Expressing ourselves in various art forms speaks to our abilities to find things that can be helpful in bringing forth our individual voice. This integrated approach to meeting our creative needs does not only include a restorative component, but it is foremost a sensory-based and action-oriented communication with an open-ended possibility of continued joy as we never stop learning on our road filled with surprises and deeper creative insights.

From the exercises in this book, you can now build on what you have experienced. Make a monthly date with yourself where you continue building on your creative portfolio as you stride deeper and deeper into the web of relationships reemerging through play and your own artful lens. In *The House at Pooh*

Corner, A. A. Milne wrote: "Wherever they go, and whatever happens to them on the way, in that enchanted forest, a little boy and his Bear will always be playing."

In our aging process filled with accumulated experiences, we will find how important play and joy are to our overall well-being, and we can always keep playing in our imaginary and enchanted forest.

Credits

“Ich lebe mein Leben . . . /I live my life in widening” by Rainer Maria Rilke, copyright © 1996 by Anita Barrows & Joanna Macy; from RILKE’S BOOK OF HOURS: LOVE POEMS TO GOD by Rainer Maria Rilke, translated by Anita Barrows and Joanna Macy. Used by permission of Riverhead, an imprint of Penguin Publishing Group, a division of Penguin Random House LLC. All rights reserved.

“The Journey” from DREAM WORK: POEMS by Mary Oliver, copyright © 1986 by NW Orchard LLC. Used by permission of Penguin Books, an imprint of Penguin Publishing Group, a division of Penguin Random House LLC. All rights reserved.

“Her Grave” by Mary Oliver Reprinted by the permission of The Charlotte Sheedy Literary Agency as agent for the author. Copyright © 1992, 2006, 2013 by Mary Oliver with permission of Bill Reichblum.

Galileo’s Riddle by Roberto Márquez reprinted with permission of the artist.

Sources

Bainbridge Cohen, Bonnie. *Sensing, Feeling, and Action: The Experiential Anatomy of Body-Mind Centering.* Middletown, CT: Wesleyan University Press, 2018.

Beveridge, Charles E., and Paul Rocheleau. *Frederick Law Olmsted: Designing the American Landscape*. New York: Rizzoli International Publications, 2005.

Campbell, Joseph. *The Hero with a Thousand Faces.* Princeton, NJ: Princeton University Press, 1949.

Carson, Rachel. *The Sense of Wonder.* New York: Harpers & Row, 1956.

Charon, Rita. *Narrative Medicine: Honoring the Stories of Illness.* New York: Oxford University Press, 2008.

Cohen, Gene D. "Research on Creativity and Aging; The Positive Impact of the Arts on Health and Illness." *A Journal of the American Society of Aging* 30, no. 1 (2006): 7–15.

Csikszentmihalyi, Mihaly. *Flow: The Psychology of Optimal Experience.* New York: Harper & Row, 1990.

Dissanayake, Ellen. *What Is Art For?* Seattle: University of Washington Press, 1988.

Dissanayake, Ellen. *Art and Intimacy: How the Arts Began*. Seattle: University of Washington Press, 2000.

Hillman, James. *The Soul's Code.* New York: Warner Books, 1996

Holland, Jimmie C., and Sheldon Lewis. *The Human Side of Cancer.* New York: Harper Collins, 2001.

Hollis, James. *Finding Meaning in the Second Half of Life: How to Finally Really Grow Up.* New York: Avery, 2006.

Jung, Carl. *Memories, Dreams, Reflections.* Edited by Aniela Jaffé. Translated by Richard and Clara Winston. New York: Vintage Books, 1989.

Keltner, Dacher, and Jonathan Haidt. "Approaching Awe: A Moral, Spiritual, and Aesthetic Emotion." *Cognition and Emotion* 17, no. 2 (2003): 297–314.

Kübler-Ross, Elisabeth. *On Death and Dying.* New York: Macmillan, 1969.

Lazarus, Richard S. *Stress and Emotion.* New York: Springer, 2006.

Maddux, James E. "Self-Efficacy: The Power of Believing You Can." In *Handbook of Positive Psychology*, edited by C. R. Snyder and Shane J. Lopez, 277–287. New York: Oxford University Press, 2005.

May, Rollo. *The Courage to Create.* New York: W.W. Norton & Company, 1975

Meade, Michael. "*The Necessity of Gratitude.*" *Living Myth Podcast*. November 26, 2024. https://www.mosaicvoices.org/episode-411-the-necessity-of-gratitude

Nin, Anais. *The Diary of Anais Nin, Vol 3, (1939-1944).* New York: Harcourt Brace Jovanovich, Inc. 1969.

Nobel, Jeremy. "Alleviating Loneliness in Older Adults Through Creative Expression." *Generations Journal* 1 (2024): 21–32.

O'Donohue, John. *Beauty: The Invisible Embrace.* New York: Harper Collins, 2003.

Peck, M. Scott. *The Road Less Traveled.* New York: Touchstone, 1978.

Pert, Candace B. *Molecules of Emotion: Why You Feel the Way You Feel.* New York: Scribner, 1998.

Plotkin, Bill. *Nature and the Human Soul.* Novato: New World Library, 2008.

Rilke, Rainer M. *The Selected Poems of Rainer Maria Rilke.* Translated by Robert Bly. New York: Harper & Row, 1981.

Rumi, Jeladaden. *The Essential Rumi.* Translated by Coleman Barks. New York: Harper Collins, 1995.

Ryff, Carol D., and Susan M. Heidrich. "Experience and Well-Being: Explorations on Domains of Life and How They Matter."

International Journal of Behavioral Development 20, no. 2 (1997): 193–206.

Sagan, Carl. *The Demon-Haunted World.* New York: Random House, 1995.

Stein, Helen. "Does Mentalizing Promote Resilience?" In *Handbook of Mentalization-Based Treatment*, edited by J. G. Allen and P. Fonagy, 307–326. New York: John Wiley & Sons, 2006.

Suleika, Jaouad. *Between Two Kingdoms: What Almost Dying Taught Me About Living.* New York: Penguin, 2022.

Tolle, Eckhart. *A New Earth: Awakening to Your Life's Purpose.* New York: Penguin Group, 2006.

Walsh, Diana Chapman. "The Tension of Opposites." *Medium,* September 2, 2023. https:// medium.com.

Walpole, Hugh. *Reading: An Essay.* New York: Harper & Bros, 1927.

Weir, Kirsten. "The Science Behind Creativity." *APA Journal Monitor on Psychology* 53, no. 3 (2022): 40–46.

Whyte, David. *The Bell and the Blackbird.* Washington: Many Rivers Press, 2018

Winnicott, Donald W. *Playing and Reality*. New York: Pavistock Publications, 1971.

Wohlleben, Peter. *The Hidden Life of Trees.* London: Harper Collins, 2016.

Acknowledgments

Writing this book has been a journey of creativity, reflection, and deep gratitude. I want to express my sincere appreciation to the many people I have encountered along the way. Without their encouragement, wisdom, and support, these pages would not have been possible.

First and foremost, I extend my heartfelt gratitude to the older adults, clients, and students who have shared their creative journeys with me. Your willingness to explore new forms of expression, your courage in embracing creativity at every stage of life, and your stories of transformation have been my greatest inspiration. This book exists because of you.

To my family and dear friends—thank you for your unwavering belief in this project. Your encouragement, thoughtful conversations, and gentle reminders to take creative pauses sustained me throughout the writing process. Special thanks to Ray Fleming, Gudrun Lindgren, and Christiane Manzella for your patience and support—whether through reading early drafts, offering much-needed perspective, or simply reminding me why this work matters.

To my editor, Melinda Cross, your keen insights and careful guidance helped shape this book into its best form. Your understanding of storytelling and creative expression has been invaluable. I am also deeply grateful to Anne Durette, editor at

She Writes Press, and to the entire team there for believing in this work and helping to bring it into the world.

To the artists, educators, and mentors who have influenced my thinking—thank you for sharing your knowledge and passion for creativity. A special note of gratitude to Carl Jung, whose unwavering belief in the power of creativity and the soul has been a constant source of inspiration. Your work continues to guide me and, in turn, the readers of this book.

Finally, to every reader who picks up this book with a curiosity to explore their own creativity—thank you. May this book serve as a gentle invitation to play, discover, and embrace the joy of creative expression.

About the Author

Photo courtesy of the author

BrittMarie Eksell grew up in Stockholm, Sweden, and moved to the US in 1975 to study textile design at Pratt Institute. She built a career crafting large-scale tapestries for public spaces while also teaching painting and weaving. Inspired by the power of creative expression, she earned an MA in art therapy and a PhD in health psychology and went on to work in cancer hospitals, creating spaces for emotional expression and healing. After spending 35 years in the US, she now resides in Scotland.

For additional images and creative inspiration, you can visit www.britteksell.com. There, BrittMarie invites you to share your own images and stories while bringing forth your truly human creative experience. With continued practices and additional resources, Eksell encourages you to continue finding renewed creative joy and never-ending potential.

Looking for your next great read?

We can help!

Visit www.shewritespress.com/next-read
or scan the QR code below for a list
of our recommended titles.